The Actor's

Molière

Volume 3

SCAPIN

and

DON JUAN

in new translations by Albert Bermel

D1114418

THEATRE BOOK PUBLISHERS

211 West 71 St. New York, N.Y. 10023

Printed in U.S.A.

ISBN O-936839-80-5

Library of Congress Cataloging-in-Publication Data

Molière, 1622-1673.
[Fourberies de Scapin. English]
Scapin; and, Don Juan: in new translations / by Albert Bermel.
    p. cm. — (The Actor's Molière; v.3)
Translation of : Les Fourberies de Scapin and Don Juan.
ISBN 0-936839-80-5 (pbk.) : $5.95
1. Molière, 1622-1673 — Translations, English. 2. Don Juan (Legendary character)—Drama. I. Bermel, Albert. II. Molière, 1622-1673. Don Juan. English. 1987. III. Title. IV. Title: Scapin.
V. Title: Don Juan. VI Series: Molière, 1622-1673. Actor's Molière; v.3.
PQ1825.E5 1987c
842'.4—dc19   87-33381
                                                              CIP

CONTENTS

For Ron Moody—
onstage, the model Harpagon;
offstage, the most generous of men–
in gratitude for many years of friendship

THE SCAMS OF SCAPIN

(Les Fourberies de Scapin)

Argante, father of Octave and Zerbinette
Géronte, father of Léandre and Hyacinte
Octave, son of Argante, in love with Hyacinte
Léandre, son of Géronte, in love with Zerbinette
Zerbinette, daughter of Argante but raised by Romanies, in love
    with Léandre
Hyacinte, daughter of Géronte, in love with Octave
Scapin, Léandre's valet, a trickster
Silvestre, Octave's valet
Nérine, Hyacinte's nurse
Carle, another trickster

The play takes place in Naples.

ACT ONE

The street, not far from the houses of Argante, Géronte, and Nérine.

Octave and Silvestre.

OCTAVE   Hard news for a tender heart, Silvestre.   Bleak prospects! I'm stuck, I'm trapped, I'm baffled.   And you found out at the harbor that my father has returned?

SILVESTRE   Returned, yes.

OCTAVE   He docks this morning?

SILVESTRE   This morning.

OCTAVE   And he's determined to marry me off?

SILVESTRE   Yes.

OCTAVE   To Géronte's daughter?

SILVESTRE   Géronte's, yes.

OCTAVE   And he's shipping the girl here from Taranto?

SILVESTRE   Yes, from Taranto.

OCTAVE   You heard this from my uncle?

SILVESTRE   From your uncle.

OCTAVE   Who received a letter from my father?

SILVESTRE   Yes, a letter.

OCTAVE   And my uncle knows everything we've done.

SILVESTRE   Everything we've done.

OCTAVE   If you have something to say, say it. Stop being a
ventriloquist's dummy and plucking words out of my mouth.

SILVESTRE   What can I add? All this hot news you're passing on to
me I just passed on to you. You didn't overlook one detail.

OCTAVE   Make a few brilliant suggestions. How do I break out of
this bind?

SILVESTRE   I'm as bamboozled as you. I could use a few
suggestions myself.

OCTAVE   He's done me in by coming back now.

SILVESTRE   And me.

OCTAVE   Once he knows how things stand, he'll break out in a
storm of indignation.

SILVESTRE   Indignation! If it would only stop there! He'll blame
me for your folly and break out in thunderbolts, all over my lower
back.

OCTAVE   I'm up to my ears in this mess. Can't I climb out?

SILVESTRE   You should have thought of that before you jumped in.

OCTAVE   Ah, you make me sick with your preaching.

SILVESTRE   You make me even sicker with your stupidity.

OCTAVE   What can I do? Which way can I turn? Where's the
answer?

Enter Scapin.

SCAPIN   The answer to what? You look all downcast and
disorderly, master Octave. Is something wrong?

OCTAVE   I'm lost, Scapin. I'm desperate. I'm suicidal.

SCAPIN   Why?

OCTAVE   Haven't you heard anything?

SCAPIN   No.

OCTAVE   About my father's arrival with Géronte?   They want me to marry.

SCAPIN   Is that so sad?

OCTAVE   Sad! I'm lost, desperate.

SYLVESTRE   Suicidal.

OCTAVE   And you can't guess why?

SCAPIN   I'll make a shrewd guess if you tell me first. I'm a helpful sort. I take an interest in young men who are lost, desperate, and suicidal.

OCTAVE   If you can only do something for me, come up with a miracle, an idea that's unbeatable, undefeatable, I'll owe you more than my life for the rest of my life.

SCAPIN   Well now, practically nothing is impossible when you know what you're about. And I do. Call it genius if you like. But when it comes to what vulgar people look on as lies, intrigues, dirty tricks, swindles, and similar honorable pursuits, I can say without bragging that I'm the craftiest craftsman in the world. And the most famous. But not enough people appreciate those skills nowadays, and I gave them up after a particular experience.

OCTAVE   What kind of experience?

SCAPIN   A brush with the law.

SYLVESTRE   You never told me about any brush.

SCAPIN   Oh yes. We had our differences.

SYLVESTRE   You and the law?

SCAPIN   Yes. Didn't treat me at all fairly. I said to myself, "This is an ungrateful century. I won't do another thing for it." Anyway ... Go on with what you were saying.

OCTAVE   Remember how, two months ago, my father and Géronte sailed off on that business trip?

SCAPIN   Of course.

OCTAVE   And how they left you in charge of Léandre and Silvestre here in charge of me?

SCAPIN   Yes, and I did a first-rate job.

OCTAVE   Shortly after, Léandre fell in love with that gypsy girl.

SCAPIN   I know that too.

OCTAVE   Then it all began.

SCAPIN   What began?

OCTAVE   My predicament. We're close friends and he told me he was in love with her and took me to meet her. Yes, she wasn't bad-looking, but nothing like as ravishing as he wanted me to believe. He talked about her, and nothing but her, every day. Gross exaggerations! So beautiful, so intelligent, a charmer, a great conversationalist. He reported every word she spoke, and continually reminded me how sharp-witted she was. And he kept on at me for not responding sensitively enough.

SCAPIN   What does this have to do with your predicament?

OCTAVE   One day Léandre and I were about to visit the people who guard the gypsy girl when we heard someone crying and sobbing. We went into this small house and there we witnessed the most heartrending scene. An old lady lay dying. A servant knelt nearby moaning prayers, and next to the bed stood a young woman in tears, the most beautiful and affecting girl you can imagine and as for her tears —

SCAPIN   Aha!

OCTAVE   I don't exaggerate. Not a bit.

SCAPIN   How could you?

OCTAVE   In her plight, somebody else would have made a ridiculous impression, because all she had on was a mischievous little skirt with a simple cotton pajama top, and a yellow band that let her hair fall below her shoulders. But she looked so gorgeous, so fascinating, so ravishing that if I went into each wonderful particular —

SCAPIN   No need to. I can guess what's coming.

OCTAVE   Scapin, if you'd only seen her, you'd have been bowled over.

SCAPIN   I'm bowled over without seeing her.

OCTAVE   Those tears of hers, for instance. They were not ugly tears, the kind that disfigure a face. She wept like an angel — the finest tears I ever studied, diamonds that caught the meager light and refracted it brilliantly.

SCAPIN   I can see them.

OCTAVE   Then she fell upon the body of the dying woman, crying, "Oh, mother, dear mother!" Everyone present felt pangs of sympathy and admiration, she did it so unselfconsciously.

SCAPIN   And that's why you fell in love with her.

OCTAVE   Scapin, I swear a wild beast would have fallen in love with her.

SCAPIN   How could he stop himself?

OCTAVE   We left after I'd spoken a few words of consolation to this irresistible creature, and I asked Léandre what he thought of her. He said he thought she wasn't bad-looking. I was so put off by his chilly manner that I didn't tell him her beauty had struck me to the soul.

SILVESTRE   If you don't cut this recital short, we'll be here till tomorrow. Let me finish it off fast. Then and there he catches fire. Can't live without her. Keeps running back to see her. But the mother dies and the servant won't let him in. Anguish! Torments! He begs, pleads, beseeches. Nothing doing. He learns that his beloved has no income but does come from a respectable family. He can't woo her till he marries her. The complications of love! He worries, deliberates, debates with himself, makes up his mind. So here he is: three days married.

SCAPIN I follow.

SILVESTRE Now his father arrives home suddenly, instead of staying away for another two months. He wants Octave to marry the daughter of Géronte by a woman in Taranto.

OCTAVE Add to that my poor darling's poverty. And I don't have what it takes to help her out.

SCAPIN Is that all? Do I see the two of you flattened, destroyed, for no reason? That alarms me, that does. Aren't you ashamed of yourself, Silvestre, a great lout like you? Can't you squeeze one idea from that chunky head of yours, one bright little scheme to straighten everything out? I wish I'd had the chance before to put one over on those two old birds. I'd wing 'em. I'd soon bring 'em down. When I was a tot, no taller than that, I was famous for hundreds of little gags and pranks.

SILVESTRE Me, I'm not blessed with your gifts for getting on the wrong side of the law.

OCTAVE Look who's here! My dearest Hyacinte . . .

Enter Hyacinte.

HYACINTE Octave, I just heard the news about your father.

OCTAVE I know. But don't weep, my dearest. You can't believe that I'll go along with his orders? I love you as much as ever. More.

HYACINTE I'm sure of that. But for how long?

OCTAVE When I fall in love, it's always for life.

HYACINTE People tell me that men fall in love easily, and fall out even more easily.

OCTAVE But my love isn't like other men's. I'll love you feverishly until the moment I drop into my coffin.

HYACINTE   I'd like to believe you. You seem sincere. But what about your father's power? You're his dependent. He wants you to marry someone else. And if you do, I'll die.

OCTAVE   I won't. He can't force me to go back on my promise to you. I'll give up my country, I'll give up my life, rather than give you up. Although I haven't seen this other woman, I loathe her. I don't want to be cruel, but I wish she'd disappear into the ocean. You see, there's no reason for you to cry. Please don't. It wounds me.

HYACINTE   Very well. I'll dry my eyes and look forward to whatever the future brings.

OCTAVE   It will bring us happiness.

HYACINTE   It will, it will, if you remain faithful.

OCTAVE   I swear it.

HYACINTE   Then I swear I'll be happy.

SCAPIN   *(Aside)* She's no fool. And quite a beauty.

OCTAVE   This is Scapin. He has fabulous talents. And he's going to help us.

SCAPIN   I swore an oath never to get involved with people again. But if the two of you ask me nicely . . .

OCTAVE   Is that all? Then I beg you to take over and guide us.

SCAPIN   *(To Hyacinte)* And you, what do you have to say?

HYACINTE   I implore you, as he does, by whatever you hold dearest, to come to our help.

SCAPIN   I took an oath, but there's no point in being stubborn. Good. I'm on your side.

OCTAVE   I assure you —

SCAPIN   Enough. *(To Hyacinte)* Go off and relax. *(To Octave)* And you, prepare to meet your maker.

OCTAVE   What? To die?

SCAPIN   No, to face your father.

OCTAVE   I couldn't. I'm timid by nature. Can't help it.

SCAPIN   If you don't appear resolute right off, he'll spot your
weakness and treat you like a child. Steady yourself for a moment.
Answer his questions firmly.

OCTAVE   I'll do what I can.

SCAPIN   Let's rehearse. Ready? Bold face, head up, confidence!

OCTAVE   Like so?

SCAPIN   More yet.

OCTAVE   This?

SCAPIN   Better. Now, I'll be your father. Don't forget: stand up
to me. . . "What's been going on, you worthless brat? Do you
dare look me brazenly in the eye after what you've done behind my
back? Is this what I get in return for being a loving father? The
respect, the devotion you owe me?" Come on: say something!

"You have the nerve to contract a marriage without my consent, a
secret marriage? I want an answer, you cheat. An answer! Defend
yourself!" Ah, what the hell's the use? You're dumbstruck.

OCTAVE   You sound too fatherly.

SCAPIN   You look too cowardly.

OCTAVE   I'm over that now. I'll be my usual self: bold, firm.

SCAPIN   You're sure?

OCTAVE   Sure.

SCAPIN   Good. Here's your father.

OCTAVE   God, I'm desperate, I'm lost.

SILVESTRE   Suicidal.

Octave takes off rapidly.

SCAPIN   Hold it! Octave! He's gone. Some poor specimen he is! Silvestre, it's up to us. We can tackle the old man, can't we?

SILVESTRE   What do I tell him?

SCAPIN   I'll do the talking.

Enter Argante, chatting to himself. Silvestre and Scapin move out of sight.

ARGANTE   Whoever heard of a situation like this?

SCAPIN   He's found out.

SILVESTRE   I know.

SCAPIN   And it's bugging him so badly he's squabbling with himself.

ARGANTE   The audacity!

SCAPIN   Listen to the old clunk.

ARGANTE   I can't wait to hear what they say about this marriage.

SCAPIN   You won't wait long.

ARGANTE   Most likely they'll try to deny it.

SCAPIN   No. We have other ideas.

ARGANTE   Or they'll invent some excuses.

SCAPIN   That's more like it.

ARGANTE   Or mislead me with fancy stories.

SCAPIN   Even more likely.

ARGANTE   Whatever they say, I won't listen.

SCAPIN   We'll soon see.

ARGANTE   They can't fool me.

SCAPIN   Don't bet on it.

ARGANTE   I could have that wicked son of mine locked up.

SCAPIN   We've thought of that.

ARGANTE   And that Silvestre, I'll whip him to a pulp.

SILVESTRE   Dear old soul — I knew he wouldn't forget me.

Scapin and Silvestre make themselves visible.

ARGANTE   Silvestre! Some fine guardian you turned out to be!

SCAPIN   I'm delighted to welcome you home, monsieur.

ARGANTE   Good morning, Scapin. Silvestre, is this how you follow my orders while I'm away? Is this how you encourage my son to behave?

SCAPIN   Sir, you look uncommonly well.

ARGANTE   Fairly well. Silvestre, why don't you answer me?

SCAPIN   And how was the trip? Nice?

ARGANTE   Very nice. Good God, let me pick on him in peace.

SCAPIN   You want to pick on him?

ARGANTE   I do. Very much.

SCAPIN   How come?

ARGANTE   Haven't you heard what happened while I was not here?

SCAPIN   I did hear of some small thing.

ARGANTE   Small thing! What, an enormous thing like that?

SCAPIN   I see what you mean.

ARGANTE   An act of sheer defiance?

SCAPIN   In a way.

ARGANTE   A boy who marries without his father's permission?

SCAPIN   There's more to it than that. But I wouldn't bother about it if I were you.

ARGANTE   Not bother? I intend to bother with all my might. Don't I have every right to lose my temper?

SCAPIN   I suppose so. I lost mine when I first heard about it, and I ticked him off, acting in your interests, of course. Ask him about the tongue-lashing I gave him and how I preached about the respect a son owes a father. I told him he ought to get down and kiss your feet. You yourself couldn't have been more brutal with him. But then I started to think. I realized that he hadn't done anything too disgraceful.

ARGANTE   Are you saying it's not disgraceful to rush into marriage with a strange girl?

SCAPIN   What do you expect? He was pushed into it by his fate.

ARGANTE   I've heard that one before. You can commit every crime imaginable — adultery, theft, murder — and then say it was the fault of fate.

SCAPIN   No, monsieur, no. You're too philosophical. You take me wrong. I meant that he got fatally mixed up in this affair.

ARGANTE   Why did he get mixed up at all?

SCAPIN   Because he's not as sensible as you. Young people are, well, young. They lack the commonsense they'd need to be reasonable. Take our Léandre. I argued with him, yelled at him. He still did something even worse than your son. And what about yourself? You got up to some fine old capers in your time. I've heard that you were quite a one with the women and plunged into one affair after another and took them all to the limit.

ARGANTE   I won't say I wasn't or didn't when I could. Or that they didn't like it. But he's gone *beyond* the limit. I never went that far.

SCAPIN   How could he help it? He sees this girl who's attracted to him, and he gets that from you, being fatally attractive to women. She's a charmer. He goes to her house, murmurs a few gallant compliments seasoned with sighs, stirs up a passion or two. You remember the sort of thing? Well, after that, she really wants him. He pushes his luck. When all of a sudden her relatives catch them together and force him to marry her.

SILVESTRE *(Aside)*   He's a wonderful liar.

SCAPIN   Should he let them kill him? Never. Better wed than dead.

ARGANTE   This is a different story from the one I heard.

SCAPIN   Ask Silvestre here. He'll confirm it.

ARGANTE   Silvestre, is this true? They forced him to marry her?

SILVESTRE Yes, sir.

SCAPIN   Would I lie to you?

ARGANTE   Why didn't he go off at once and speak to a lawyer?

SCAPIN   That he wouldn't do.

ARGANTE   Then it would have been easier for me to annul the marriage.

SCAPIN   You'll never annul that marriage.

ARGANTE   I won't?

SCAPIN   No.

ARGANTE   But I'm his father and they threatened him with violence.

SCAPIN   He won't let you.

ARGANTE   My own son won't let me?

SCAPIN   That's what I said. Do you want him to confess that he was scared and gave in to the threat of violence? He'll never admit that. He'd lose his reputation and damage yours.

ARGANTE   That doesn't worry me.

SCAPIN   No, for the sake of his honor, and yours, he must tell everyone that he married her willingly.

ARGANTE   Well, for the sake of his honor, and mine, I want him to say the opposite.

SCAPIN   I'm sure he won't.

ARGANTE   I'll do it by force. I'll threaten him with violence.

SCAPIN   He still won't.

ARGANTE   He will, or he'll be out of my will.

SCAPIN   No.

ARGANTE   Yes.

SCAPIN   All right.

ARGANT   What's all right about it?

SCAPIN   You won't cut him out of your will.

ARGANTE   I won't?

SCAPIN   You will — not.

ARGANTE   I like this — he tells me I won't when I will.

SCAPIN   Not a hope.

ARGANTE   Who'll stop me?

SCAPIN   You will.

ARGANTE   I won't.

SCAPIN   You'd never have the heart to.

ARGANTE   I will.

SCAPIN   You're pretending.

ARGANTE   I am not.

SCAPIN   Your fatherly affection will come into play.

ARGANTE   I won't let it.

SCAPIN   You can't prevent it.

ARGANTE   I can, I must, I will.

SCAPIN   Bullshine.

ARGANTE   No bull or any other shine.

SCAPIN   Good heavens, don't I know you? You have a sweet
personality.

ARGANTE   Not all the time. I can turn on a sour personality
whenever I wish. And this conversation is making my acid flow.
Silvestre, go! Fetch me that young sinner. I'll be with Géronte,
telling him about my bad luck.

SCAPIN   May I be of any service to you, monsieur?

ARGANTE   No thanks. *(Aside, as he leaves)* Why does he have to
be my only child? Why did I lose my daughter? I'd have settled
every stitch of my property on her. *(Exit.)*

SILVESTRE   You're a great shyster. I admit that. Things are
looking up at last. But we're still short of money. We have
creditors barking like dogs at our heels.

SCAPIN   Leave everything to me. Our plot's under way. Let me
think. What we need now is a reliable man who can carry out
instructions. Wait! Hold that pose! Pull your hat well down like a
street fighter's. Stand with one foot on the other. Slip your hand

in your pocket. Let your eyes glitter. Strut around like an actor playing a king. That's it! Now come with me and I'll let you in on some trade secrets — how to create a new face and voice.

SILVESTRE   I don't want any brushes with the law.

SCAPIN   Come on, come on! We'll share the danger, like brothers. Three years, more or less, chained to the oars in a stinking, wet galley are not enough to deter brave hearts.

ACT TWO

Géronte and Argante. The street, outside their houses.

GERONTE   Yes, if this weather holds, we'll have our people here today. A sailor from Taranto told me he saw my man ready to sail. But my daughter will arrive at the wrong time. Your son has wrecked our plans.

ARGANTE   Not to worry. I'll rescue us from that difficulty. I'm going right to work on it.

GERONTE   But look here, Argante, I'll be frank with you. A father must be strict and conscientious in educating his children.

ARGANTE   Unquestionably. What's the connection?

GERONTE   Young people behave badly when their fathers give them a bad education.

ARGANTE   Sometimes. Géronte, what are you hinting at?

GERONTE   Hinting?

ARGANTE   Yes.

GERONTE   If you'd taught your son properly he wouldn't have pulled this stunt on you.

ARGANTE   Did you teach yours much better?

GERONTE   Unquestionably. I'd get pretty mad if my boy did anything like that to me.

ARGANTE   And what if this well-taught boy of yours had done something even worse?

GERONTE   What do you mean?

ARGANTE   I mean, Géronte, that you shouldn't be so quick to find fault. Before you criticize other families, be safe and check out your own.

GERONTE   I can't make sense of what you're saying.

ARGANTE   It'll become clear.

GERONTE   Have you heard something about my son?

ARGANTE   Could be.

GERONTE   What is it, then?

ARGANTE   Your Scapin gave me the general idea. I was in a rage; I didn't listen properly. You'll have to ask him or someone else for the details. Me, I'm in a hurry to talk to a lawyer and decide on an angle. Good-by. *(Exit.)*

GERONTE   What *is* this business? Even worse than Léandre's? According to Scapin! Ha! I don't see how anything could be worse. To marry without your father's consent — unimaginable! *(Enter Léandre.)* Ah, you're here.

LEANDRE   *(Running across to embrace him)*   Welcome back, Father. I'm so happy to see you again.

GERONTE   *(Spurning the embrace)*   Hold it! I want to talk business.

LEANDRE   Let me give you a hug first, and —

GERONTE   *(Still holding him off)*   I said no.

LEANDRE   Father! You won't even accept a joyful hug?

GERONTE   Léandre, there's something we must clear up. Now!

LEANDRE   What's that?

GERONTE   Stand still. Face me.

LEANDRE   All right.

GERONTE   Look me in the eye.

LEANDRE   So?

GERONTE   What's been going on?

LEANDRE   Going on?

GERONTE   Yes. What did you get up to while I was away?

LEANDRE   What do you think I got up to?

GERONTE   Never mind what I think. I'm asking what you did.

LEANDRE   I haven't done a thing you could complain about.

GERONTE   Not one thing?

LEANDRE   Not one.

GERONTE   You're quite sure?

LEANDRE   Sure and innocent.

GERONTE   But Scapin passed on some news about you.

LEANDRE   Scapin did!

GERONTE   Aha, that name! You're blushing.

LEANDRE   Scapin?   News about me?

GERONTE   We can't talk here. We'll thrash it out later. Go indoors. I'll be back soon. If it turns out that you've disgraced me, I'll reject you as my son and never see you again. *(Exit.)*

LEANDRE   Scapin! That bigmouth! He should be the last person to blab about anything I told him in confidence. Instead, he's the first to run and tattle to my father. I'll make him suffer for this.

Enter Octave and Scapin.

OCTAVE   My dear Scapin, I'm so grateful to you. You're a splendid man. Thank God you came to my rescue.

LEANDRE   So there you are. I'm delighted to see you, you rat.

SCAPIN   Thanks for the greeting, master. You're too kind.

LEANDRE   *(Drawing his sword)*   I'll teach you to joke with me.

SCAPIN   *(On his knees)*   Master!

OCTAVE   *(Stepping between them)*   Léandre!

LEANDRE   Octave, don't stand in my way!

SCAPIN   But master!

OCTAVE   *(Holding onto Léandre)*   For heaven's sake!

LEANDRE   Let me get at him!

OCTAVE   Don't hurt him, Léandre, in the name of friendship.

SCAPIN   What did I do to you?

LEANDRE   What you did to me, you blabbermouth!

OCTAVE   *(Still holding Léandre)*   Easy now, easy!

LEANDRE   No, Octave, I want a confession from him. He betrayed me. *(To Scapin)* I know very well what you did. A dirty trick. I just heard about it. Maybe you thought it wouldn't come back to me. I want the truth out of your own loose lips or I'll run you through.

SCAPIN   No, master, you wouldn't have the heart.

LEANDRE   Confess, then.

SCAPIN   I did something or other to you?

LEANDRE   Yes, and you know what. Let your conscience speak.

SCAPIN   I honestly don't know.

LEANDRE   *(Raising his sword)*   You don't know?

OCTAVE *(Holding him again)* Léandre!

SCAPIN Good enough, master. You insist on a confession? I'll confess. That little barrel of Spanish wine somebody gave you a few days back: I shared it with some friends. Then I split the wood and spilled water all around to make you think the wine had leaked out.

LEANDRE So you drank up my Spanish wine? And I blamed the poor maid for it!

SCAPIN I'm very sorry, master.

LEANDRE I'm glad to know about this, but I'm not referring to the wine.

SCAPIN That's not it?

LEANDRE No, it's something that affects me much more seriously. Now — out with it!

SCAPIN I don't remember doing anything else.

LEANDRE *(Threatening him again)* You won't say?

SCAPIN Help!

OCTAVE Easy, easy!

SCAPIN I know. One evening about three weeks ago you gave me a watch for that gypsy girl you're in love with. I came back with my clothes all muddy and my face bloody. I told you some thieves had beaten me up and stolen the watch. Not so, master. I kept it.

LEANDRE You kept my watch?

SCAPIN I wanted to know the time.

LEANDRE We're learning some nice things here, aren't we? You're some loyal servant. But that's still not what I'm asking about.

SCAPIN That's not it, either?

LEANDRE   No, and you know what it is. Now confess!

SCAPIN   To hell with it!

LEANDRE   No more stalling. I'm in a hurry.

SCAPIN   That's all I've done, master.

LEANDRE   *(Threatening him again)*   So that's all?

OCTAVE   *(Intervening again)*   No!

SCAPIN   Except for . . . But that was six months ago. You remember the werewolf, master, who kept hitting you with a club in the darkness and you almost broke your neck when you ran away and fell into a cellar?

LEANDRE   Well?

SCAPIN   I played the werewolf.

LEANDRE   You *played* the werewolf?

SCAPIN   Yes, master, to give you a bit of a scare. And to discourage you from running us ragged all night, every night.

LEANDRE   I'll deal with these games of yours at the right time. But now I want the big confession. What did you say to my father?

SCAPIN   Your father?

LEANDRE   Yes, my father, you tongue-flapper.

SCAPIN   I haven't even seen your father since he came back.

LEANDRE   You haven't seen him?

SCAPIN   No, master.

LEANDRE   You're sure?

SCAPIN   Ask him. Confirm it.

LEANDRE   He's the one who told me.

SCAPIN I beg your pardon, but he wasn't telling the truth.

Enter Carle.

CARLE Master, bad news about the lady you love.

LEANDRE Zerbinette?

CARLE Those gypsies are taking her away. She asked me to rush back here and tell you that if you don't pay the ransom within two hours, you'll lose her forever.

LEANDRE Within two hours?

CARLE That's what she said. *(Exit.)*

LEANDRE Scapin, my friend, help me, I implore you.

SCAPIN *(Strutting away)* "Scapin, my friend." Yes, I'm your friend, now you need me.

LEANDRE Look, I forgive you for everything you confessed, and anything you didn't, even if it's worse.

SCAPIN No, no. Don't forgive me. Run me through. Kill me. I'll be ecstatic.

LEANDRE I won't take your life if you give me back mine. Save her!

SCAPIN No, go ahead. Kill me. You'll feel better.

LEANDRE You're worth too much to me. Please, please, put that genius of yours to work. It always finds an answer.

SCAPIN Dead men find no answers.

LEANDRE For God's sake, forget about all that, and start thinking up a plan.

OCTAVE Scapin, you must do something for him.

SCAPIN Can I, in all conscience, after so many insults?

LEANDRE   Please! Overlook what I said. I was angry. Be my magician!

OCTAVE   I second that.

SCAPIN   Those insults struck me to the heart.

OCTAVE   It's bad for the heart to carry a grudge.

LEANDRE   Can you spurn me like this, Scapin, just when Zerbinette and I need you most?

SCAPIN   Belittling me like that, without even a warning!

LEANDRE   I was wrong, I admit.

SCAPIN   Treating me like a a con artist, a crook, a repeat offender!

LEANDRE   I can't apologize enough.

SCAPIN   And wanting to run me through!

LEANDRE   I ask you with every fiber in my body. Look, I kneel to you, Scapin. One last plea: don't turn me down.

OCTAVE   He'll injure his knees, Scapin. You can't refuse.

SCAPIN   Get up. Next time don't be so quick-tempered.

LEANDRE   Will you assist me? Do you promise?

SCAPIN   I'll think about it.

LEANDRE   We have very little time.

SCAPIN   Don't worry about that. What's the ransom?

LEANDRE   Five hundred crowns.

SCAPIN   *(To Octave)*   And you need?

OCTAVE   Two hundred francs.

SCAPIN   I'll wheedle the money out of your fathers. *(To Octave)*
In your case, things are already rolling. *(To Léandre)*   In yours, the
old boy's a miser to the nth, but he'll be even easier to handle
because he doesn't have a great supply of brain, thank God. He'll
believe whatever you want him to. That doesn't reflect on you.
Him and you? Not the ghost of a resemblance. People call him
your father, you know, only as a matter of form.

LEANDRE   That'll do, Scapin.

SCAPIN   Good enough. That's where you draw the line. You
don't mean it, of course? *(To Octave)*   Your father's coming. I'll
start with him. Away with you both. *(To Octave)*   Tell Silvestre I
need him — in character.

Léandre and Octave leave. Enter Argante.

SCAPIN   *(Aside)*   Always talking to himself.

ARGANTE   No propriety, no consideration! Flings himself into an
engagement. These headstrong young people. . .

SCAPIN   At your service, monsieur.

ARGANTE   Good morning, Scapin.

SCAPIN   You're thinking about your son's affair.

ARGANTE   It makes me furious!

SCAPIN   Life is full of letdowns, monsieur. Be prepared! I
remember some ancient words of wisdom I heard long ago.

ARGANTE   What?

SCAPIN   When a father has been away from his family for even a
short time he must turn over in his mind all the terrible accidents he
could return to — picture his house burned down, his money stolen,
his wife dead, his son a cripple, his daughter raped. Then whatever
didn't happen to him seems like good luck. Me, I always take this
advice to heart in my humble, thoughtful way. When I come home
I expect the worst from my masters — rages, reproaches, threats,
even physical damage from kicks in the butt and sticks and straps.
And if any of them don't happen, I thank my lucky stars.

ARGANTE Yes, yes, but this outrageous marriage interferes with the other one we've arranged and I won't put up with it. I've just spoken to some lawyers. I'm going to dissolve it.

SCAPIN Good God! Listen to me, monsieur: straighten things out in some other fashion. You know what lawsuits are. You'll dive headfirst into a pile of prickles.

ARGANTE I'm aware of that, but what other options are there?

SCAPIN I think I've come up with one. My sympathy for you made me wonder: how could I pull you out of this mess? It troubles me when I see kind fathers embarrassed by their children, and let's face it, I've always had a special affection for you.

ARGANTE Much obliged.

SCAPIN You're welcome. So I went to talk to the girl's brother. He's a professional thug, always waiting for the chance to put his sword into a nearby stomach or snap a spine in two. He'll have no more misgivings about murdering you than snatching the wine off your table and downing it. I got talking about this marriage and made him see how you could legally dissolve it by pleading coercion and your rights and privileges as a father, not to mention your reputation in the community and in court and your money and friends. I muddled him up until he was glad to listen when I proposed a financial settlement. Give him the agreed sum and he's willing.

ARGANTE How much did he ask?

SCAPIN At first: the ceiling, the roof, the sky.

ARGANTE Then?

SCAPIN Still much too high.

ARGANTE And?

SCAPIN He'll accept no less than five or six hundred francs.

ARGANTE I'd like to give him five or six hundred diseases. Does this comedian take me for an idiot?

SCAPIN That's what I said. I turned him down flat, made it clear you were nobody's fool. In the end, after we argued back and forth, it came down to this. He said, "I've joined the army. I need equipment, I mean the cash for it. That's why I'll let you pay me off. A fairly good horse will cost me at least sixty francs."

ARGANTE Sixty? Fine.

SCAPIN "Plus harness and pistols. Another twenty."

ARGANTE Eighty altogether.

SCAPIN Correct.

ARGANTE I can't afford it. But if I must . . .

SCAPIN "My servant also needs a horse," he says, "a cheap one. Thirty francs."

ARGANTE The hell with him! Let them both walk. Now he'll get nothing.

SCAPIN Monsieur!

ARGANTE No, he's a thief.

SCAPIN You don't expect his servant to gallop on foot?

ARGANTE For all I care, they can both gallop on their heads.

SCAPIN Don't hold back now, monsieur. It's not much more. If you put yourself in the jaws of the lawyers they'll chew you dry.

ARGANTE Oh God. All right. Add the thirty francs.

SCAPIN "I need a mule, too," he says, "to carry —"

ARGANTE I'll see him in flames first — him and his servant and the mule. I prefer the judges.

SCAPIN Please, monsieur!

ARGANTE No, I've finished with him.

SCAPIN   But one little tiny mule.

ARGANTE   I wouldn't give him an ass.

SCAPIN   Think. . .

ARGANTE   No, it's the law for me.

SCAPIN   But think — what are you letting yourself in for? Look at all the handicaps in the legal system! The circuits! Appeals to lower and higher courts! Exhaustive forms and exhausting interviews! The beasts of prey that maul you as you pass through their claws — sergeants, prosecuting attorneys, defense attorneys, assistants, recorders, judges and their clerks! And every one of 'em can find leaks in your watertight case, and sink you. A police officer will make out a false statement that does you in and you won't even know about it. Your lawyer will gang up with the other side for a hefty consideration. Shortly before they plead your case he'll disappear from the court or, if he's there, he'll shift and shuffle and split hairs and miss the point. The registrar, just to be ornery, will file prejudicial notices and stop-clauses. The recorder's clerk will swipe documents or the recorder himself will fail to record something vital to your argument. And if you take every possible precaution and dodge around all these obstacles, you'll be stunned when the judges are turned against you by religious fanatics or girl friends. If you can, monsieur, if you only can, stay away from that pit of corruption. Going to law is hell on earth. Just thinking about it makes me want to run off into the wilderness and dive under a cactus.

ARGANTE   How much is the mule?

SCAPIN   Including the mule, the two horses, the harness, pistols, and a little something he owes his landlady, it comes to two hundred.

ARGANTE   Two hundred francs?

SCAPIN   Yes.

ARGANTE   *(Crossing the stage angrily)*   Let's go. To court.

SCAPIN   On sober reflection —

ARGANTE   To court.

SCAPIN   You're going to land yourself in —

ARGANTE   Court.

SCAPIN   In court you'll need money. Expenses for the summons,
for the writs, the registration, presentation, documentation,
procuration. Fees for your attorneys' appearances and
consultations. The costs of the right to write and rewrite the briefs,
the reports and records, copies of provisional decisions by the
registrar, sentences, arrests, controls, signatures, clerical messages,
not to mention bribes at every turn and a final sweetener for the
judges. Give this man the money and you're in the clear.

ARGANTE   But two hundred!

SCAPIN   Yes, and you'll come out ahead. I've figured out roughly
what you lose by going to law. It's one hundred fifty more than our
man is asking, and you still have to put up with the agonizing
slowness and the headaches and heartaches. Never mind two
hundred: rather than have to listen to those lawyers having fun as
they make snide cracks about me in public, I'd pay three hundred.

ARGANTE   I don't give a damn. I defy the lawyers to find anything
funny about me.

SCAPIN   Do what you think best, but in your shoes I'd run like fury
from the law.

ARGANTE   I will not give him two hundred francs.

SCAPIN   Tell him to his face. Here he is.

Enter Silvestre, disguised.

SILVESTRE   Scapin, I must meet this Argante, Octave's father.

SCAPIN   Why, monsieur?

SILVESTRE   I just heard he wants to set the law against me and put
an end to my sister's marriage.

SCAPIN   I don't know if that's what he intends to do, but he won't pay you the two hundred francs. Says it's too much.

SILVESTRE   I'll have his head! His guts! I'll snap his spine in two. Let them break me on the wheel for it.

Argante has taken refuge behind Scapin.

SCAPIN   He's a great-hearted man, monsieur. He's probably not a bit scared of you.

SILVESTRE   Not scared? Blood and death! If I had him here right now I'd give him this sword in the belly button. Who's that man?

SCAPIN   Not Argante, monsieur. Somebody else.

SILVESTRE   One of his friends?

SCAPIN   No, the opposite. His worst enemy.

SILVESTRE   His worst enemy?

SCAPIN   Positively his worst.

SILVESTRE   I'll be damned. Let me shake his mitt. So you're the enemy of that law-lover Argante?

SCAPIN   He certainly is.

SILVESTRE   *(Grabbing Argante's hand)*   Let me wring that mitt. I give you my word, I swear on my honor, by this sword, by every oath I can lay my tongue to, that before this day's over I'll grind him down to wet powder for you, the slop, the old shirtful of wind. Trust me.

SCAPIN   In these parts, monsieur, they punish violence.

SILVESTRE   I don't give a hoot. I have nothing to lose.

SCAPIN   He'll be on his guard. He has people to protect him — relatives, friends, servants.

SILVESTRE   That's what I want! Christ, that's what I'm hoping for. *(He cuts and thrusts in all directions with his sword.)*   One in

the head! One in the gizzard! I'd love to have him in front of me
now, with his protecters. I'd like to see him in the middle of thirty
of 'em, all rushing at me armed to the gills. What? You rash fools!
You dare to attack me? Me? Come on, by God! Kill! No mercy!
Defend yourself! Stand your ground! Cut, thrust, parry! Quick
foot, quick eye. Rabble, cattle, you wanted it, you've got it, a
gutful, hey? Fight back, fight back! Now — on the offensive.
This is for you, and that for you, and this for you, and one for
you. . . What, are you backing off? All thirty of you? Stand firm,
you jelly bellies, stand firm!

SCAPIN   Whoa, hold it, monsieur. Hit them, not us.

SILVESTRE   That'll teach you to mess with me. *(Exit.)*

SCAPIN   There you are. You save two hundred francs and lose
thirty-one lives. Oh well. I wish you luck.

ARGANTE   *(Trembling)*   Scapin.

SCAPIN   Pardon me?

ARGANTE   I'll give him the two hundred.

SCAPIN   Delighted to hear it, for your own sake.

ARGANTE   Let's go after him. I have the money on me.

SCAPIN   Shall I take it? It'll look strange if he meets you as
yourself after you passed for somebody else. Besides, I'm afraid
that once he sees you, he'll ask for more.

ARGANTE   Yes, but I like to see exactly where my money goes.

SCAPIN   You don't trust me.

ARGANTE   It's not that, only —

SCAPIN   Now look, monsieur, either I'm a swindler or I'm an
honest man. One or the other. Would I try to deceive you when I
have only your interests at heart, and my master's? And when your
family will soon be related to ours? If you have doubts about me,
I'll back out. Look around for somebody you trust with your
money but not your life.

ARGANTE Here, then.

SCAPIN No, monsieur, I wouldn't touch it. I'll feel better if you find somebody else.

ARGANTE Take it, take it!

SCAPIN No, I said. Don't trust me. Perhaps I'm going to walk off with the whole two hundred?

ARGANTE I told you: take it! Let's not quibble any further. *(Scapin takes the purse.)* But you'll have to get some sort of security.

SCAPIN Let me handle that. He's not dealing with a halfwit.

ARGANTE I'll be home waiting for you.

SCAPIN I'll see you there. *(Exit Argante.)* One down, one to go. Well, well, here's number two. Heaven is leading them into my net. *(When Géronte enters, Scapin is looking the other way.)* A catastrophe! A tragedy! Who could have expected it? That poor father! Oh, Géronte, what can you do?

GERONTE What's he saying about me? *(Studying the back of Scapin's head)* With that gloomy face.

SCAPIN Somebody, help me find Monsieur Géronte!

GERONTE Scapin, what is it?

SCAPIN *(Searching the back of the stage)* I must let him know about this calamity.

GERONTE Why? What's wrong?

SCAPIN I've looked everywhere. Can't locate him.

GERONTE I'm here!

SCAPIN He must have gone into hiding. In some secret nook.

GERONTE Hey, are you blind? Can't you hear me?

SCAPIN   Ah, monsieur, I can't find you anywhere.

GERONTE   I've been in front of you for an hour. What's the matter?

SCAPIN   Monsieur . . .

GERONTE   Yes?

SCAPIN   Your son, monsieur . . .

GERONTE   Yes? My son?

SCAPIN   . . . Is in terrible trouble, more dangerous than you can imagine.

GERONTE   What?

SCAPIN   He was miserable on account of something you said to him, and you had me involved in it, although I wasn't, so to cheer him up we took a stroll around the harbor. Among other things there, we couldn't help noticing an elaborate Turkish galley. A friendly young Turk greeted us and asked us aboard. We went. He was extremely gracious: gave us a meal — wonderful fruits of all kinds and the finest wine I ever tasted.

GERONTE   You call that terrible trouble?

SCAPIN   I'm coming to that. During the meal, the galley took off. As soon as we were well out to sea, he sent me ashore in a skiff to report that unless you send me right back with five hundred crowns, he'll kidnap your son and keep him in Algiers.

GERONTE   That much? Five hundred crowns?

SCAPIN   Yes, monsieur. Within two hours.

GERONTE   That wicked Turk, he wants to ruin me.

SCAPIN   But your son, monsieur, your beloved boy, in chains! A galley slave! How can we save him?

GERONTE   Why the hell did he go aboard that galley?

SCAPIN   He didn't dream this could happen.

GERONTE   Go back, Scapin, make it quick, and tell that Turk I'll have the law on him.

SCAPIN   The law? On the open seas? You're joking.

GERONTE   Why the hell did he go aboard that galley?

SCAPIN   Unkind fate.

GERONTE   Scapin, this is a test of your loyalty.

SCAPIN   How come?

GERONTE   Tell the Turk to send my son home and you take his place until I scrape the money together.

SCAPIN   Think what you're saying, monsieur! This Turk's no idiot. He'll never accept a bad risk like me.

GERONTE   Why the hell did he go aboard that galley?

SCAPIN   How could he know in advance? Don't forget, monsieur, we have only two hours.

GERONTE   He's asking what?

SCAPIN   Five hundred crowns.

GERONTE   Five hundred crowns! He has no conscience.

SCAPIN   He has the conscience of a Turk.

GERONTE   Doesn't he understand how much that is?

SCAPIN   Yes, monsieur, he understands that five hundred crowns are the same as fifteen hundred francs.

GERONTE   The hog! Does he think I keep fifteen hundred francs in my pocket?

SCAPIN   Some people are unreasonable.

GERONTE But why the hell did he go aboard that galley?

SCAPIN True, but so what? He's not a fortuneteller. Please, monsieur, hurry!

GERONTE Here's the key to my closet.

SCAPIN Good.

GERONTE Open it.

SCAPIN Very good.

GERONTE On the left you'll find the large key to my attic.

SCAPIN Yes?

GERONTE The hamper up there is full of ah, slightly-worn clothing. Sell the lot to a ragpicker and take the proceeds to pay for my son.

SCAPIN *(Handing him back the key)* You're dreaming, monsieur. I wouldn't get twenty francs for the lot. Besides, we don't have enough time.

GERONTE But why the hell did he go aboard that galley?

SCAPIN You're wasting your words. Drop the galley! Time's passing. You'll lose your son. Oh, my poor master, I may never set eyes on you again! They're shipping you all the way to North Africa. As heaven is my witness, I've done what I could. If you remain in slavery for the rest of your life, it'll be because your father didn't love you enough.

GERONTE Wait, Scapin. I'll get the money.

SCAPIN Hurry, then, monsieur. I'm terrified. We must beat the clock.

GERONTE You said four hundred crowns?

SCAPIN Five hundred crowns.

GERONTE Five hundred!

SCAPIN   Yes.

GERONTE   Why the hell did he go aboard that galley?

SCAPIN   You're right, but please hurry.

GERONTE   Wasn't there anywhere else to walk?

SCAPIN   Maybe, but let's see some action.

GERONTE   That goddam galley!

SCAPIN   He's obsessed with the galley.

GERONTE   Here, Scapin, I just remembered that somebody gave me that exact amount in gold. I didn't dream it would be kidnapped. *(He offers his purse, without letting go of it.)*   Take it and set my son free.

SCAPIN   *(Reaching for the purse)*   Yes, monsieur.

GERONTE   *(Withdrawing the purse)*   And tell that Turk he's contemptible.

SCAPIN   *(Same business)*   Yes.

GERONTE   *(Same business)*   Despicable.

SCAPIN   Yes.

GERONTE   Immoral, obscene.

SCAPIN   I will.

GERONTE   He's stealing my five hundred crowns.

SCAPIN   Yes.

GERONTE   And he'd better pay them back soon.

SCAPIN   I'll mention that.

GERONTE   Or I'll have my revenge.

SCAPIN   I'll tell him.

Having repeatedly withdrawn the purse from Scapin, Gèronte now puts it back in his pocket.

GERONTE   *(Going)*   Hurry, then, hurry! Set my son free.

SCAPIN   *(Following him)*   Wait.

GERONTE   What?

SCAPIN   The money.

GERONTE   I gave it to you.

SCAPIN   You put it in your pocket.

GERONTE   I'm overwhelmed. I'm in mourning.

SCAPIN   I notice.

GERONTE   Why the hell did he go aboard that galley? That goddam galley! That contemptible, diabolical Turk! *(Exit.)*

SCAPIN   He can't get over the five hundred crowns, but we're still not even. He lied about me to his son. For that he'll pay in a different currency.

Enter Octave and Léandre.

OCTAVE   Scapin, any luck?

LEANDRE   Anything for me?

SCAPIN   For you, two hundred francs I wormed out of your father.

OCTAVE   Now I can live again!

SCAPIN   For you, not a thing.

LEANDRE   *(Leaving)*   I may as well die. I can't go on without Zerbinette.

SCAPIN   Hold it! You're in too much of a rush.

LEANDRE   There's nothing else for it.

SCAPIN   *(Showing him the purse)*   This is for you.

LEANDRE   *(Reaching for the purse)*   Now I can live again!

SCAPIN   *(Withdrawing the purse)*   But on one condition. You have to let me get my own back on your father. He lied about me.

LEANDRE   Whatever you want.

SCAPIN   You swear in front of this witness?

LEANDRE   I swear.

SCAPIN   Take it. Five hundred crowns.

LEANDRE   At last! Zerbinette will be free! And mine!

ACT THREE

Zerbinette, Hyacinte, Scapin, Silvestre.

SILVESTRE Our masters told us it'll be better for you, Zerbinette, if you stay here with Hyacinte.

HYACINTE I'm only too pleased to have your company, Zerbinette, and I'll make it as easy as I can for us to become friends, like our sweethearts.

ZERBINETTE So will I. I never resist an offer of friendship.

SCAPIN How about an offer of love?

ZERBINETTE Love? Not the same. It's a little riskier. I don't give it away so readily.

SCAPIN I can see that. But what my master has just sacrificed on your behalf deserves an equal sacrifice from you.

ZERBINETTE I'm grateful to him, of course. But has he done enough? I'm cheerful by nature; I laugh all the time. But I take some things seriously, and your master is jumping the gun if he believes that when he buys my freedom he owns me. He'll have to pay out more than money. If he wants that sacrifice from me, he'll need to make a heartfelt pledge and follow it with the usual ceremonies.

SCAPIN He appreciates that. His intentions are fair and honorable. If he had any other ideas he wouldn't have been able to count on the help of a man like me.

ZERBINETTE I believe you, if you say so; but his father may give us a hard time.

SCAPIN I'll manage him.

HYACINTE We have much in common, Zerbinette, to strengthen our friendship — a similar plight, similar hopes, similar fears.

ZERBINETTE   You have at least the advantage of knowing who your parents were. Once you find them both again you'll have them to depend on and make you happy when they approve of your marriage. But it wouldn't do me any good to discover who I am, and my present poverty doesn't recommend me to a father who wants a fat dowry.

HYACINTE   You have a different advantage. Your lover is not being tempted to marry a rival.

ZERBINETTE   I'm not so much afraid he'll have a change of heart. I think I know, in all modesty, how to hold on to him. It's his father's influence that frightens me. Compared with that, I feel powerless.

HYACINTE   It's not fair. When two people are in love, why should they face an uphill struggle? Love would be so wonderful if there were no interference.

SCAPIN   You can't mean that. A calm love affair is like a calm ocean — flat. And happiness all around is boring. We need highs and lows in life. It's the obstacles to love that make it exciting and delightful.

ZERBINETTE   Why don't you tell us the story, Scapin, of how you extracted the money from your old skinflint? I hear it's funny. You won't waste your effort. I'm a very responsive listener.

SCAPIN   Silvestre here knows it as well as I do. I'm thinking up a little act of revenge I hope to enjoy.

SILVESTRE   Why do you want to get up to more mischief — and into more trouble?

SCAPIN   I revel in taking risks.

SILVESTRE   I've already advised you not to go any further.

SCAPIN   I follow my own advice.

SILVESTRE   What the devil do you have in mind?

SCAPIN   What the devil do you care?

SILVESTRE You're taking chances, asking for a beating.

SCAPIN It'll rattle down on my rump, not yours.

SILVESTRE Why do I try to protect you from yourself? You're the boss of your own rump.

SCAPIN The fear of a beating never stopped me. I *like* taking chances and despise people who don't because they're scared of painful consequences.

ZERBINETTE But we need you.

SCAPIN Go inside. I'll join you before long. *(The others leave.)* I don't give away plans that ought to be kept secret — unless somebody puts on the pressure.

Enter Géronte.

GERONTE Scapin, is my son all right?

SCAPIN Your son is fine, monsieur. I wish you were as safe as he is. If only you'd stayed indoors! You're in grave danger.

GERONTE How grave?

SCAPIN They're hunting you down. To kill you.

GERONTE Me?

SCAPIN Yes.

GERONTE Who is?

SCAPIN The girl's brother. He thinks you want to get rid of his sister so you can marry Octave to your daughter. He swears his reputation's at stake, and the only answer is to kill you. He recruited his pals, swordsmen like him, to look all over for you, ask questions, and track you down. They've sealed off the approaches to your house. You'll never get back inside. You couldn't take six paces without falling into their hands.

GERONTE Scapin, my dear friend, what can I do?

SCAPIN I wish I knew, monsieur. This is awful. I tremble for you from head to toe, and — Hush! *(He goes to the wings and listens.)*

GERONTE Wh-what?

SCAPIN No. Nothing.

GERONTE Is there no way out for me? No plan?

SCAPIN I can think of one, yes, but I might get beaten up.

GERONTE You're used to beatings. You're such an enterprising servant. Don't run out on me now, please!

SCAPIN I never would. I'm too devoted to you. I couldn't leave you defenseless.

GERONTE You'll have your reward. I promise you this jacket as soon as I've worn it out.

SCAPIN Listen then, here's what I suggest. You pop into this sack, and —

GERONTE Who was that?

SCAPIN Where? Nobody. As I say, crawl in here and don't move a finger. I'll haul you on my back, like a bundle of something, past your attackers and into the house. Once we're there, we'll barricade ourselves inside and send for a rescue party.

GERONTE Good idea.

SCAPIN The best. You'll see. *(Aside)* I'll pay you back for that lie.

GERONTE What?

SCAPIN I said we'll pay them back by and by. Squeeze yourself right down to the bottom. They mustn't see you and you mustn't budge, whatever happens.

GERONTE *(Entering the sack)* Trust me. I won't even shiver.

SCAPIN Keep down! Here's one of them, a real roughneck.

(He imitates footsteps approaching, then puts on a foreign accent and answers in his own voice.)
–Whan ay fine thees Hayrontay, ay keel heem. Whar he gone?
–*(To Géronte)* Don't move!
–Eef he croll to meedle of zhe ert, ay deeg heem up.
–*(To Géronte)* Stay down! Don't let him see you.
–You, thar! Man weez sack!
–Yes, monsieur?
–Ay geeb you beeg monnay eef you tal me whar ees Hayrontay.
–You're looking for Monsieur Géronte?
–Si, si, ay looking for heem.
–What do you want with him, monsieur?
–What ay want?
–Yes.
–Only ay want beat heem to dead weez my steeck.
–That's not right. You can't beat a gentleman like him to death. It's not civilized.
–Zhentleman? Zees eedeeott ob a Hayrontay, zees dog, zees scom?
–Let me inform you that he is not an idiot, a dog, or scum. And you'd better keep a civil tongue in your head when you speak of Monsieur Géronte.
–What zees? You tal me what I do?
–He's a man of honor, and I'd defend him with my life.
–You be a frand ob Hayrontay?
–Yes, I am his friend.
–Bueno, you be hees frand, ay geeb you geeft for heem. *(He whacks away at the sack with his stick.)* How you like zees?
–Oh, oh, oo, ow, oh, ow! Please, monsieur, stop, ow, no, no, monsieur!
–You geeb heem thees from me. Adios.
(He imitates retreating footsteps, then doubles up as if he'd been beaten.)
–Oh, ow, that dirty foreigner! He's crippled me.

GERONTE *(His head emerging from the sack)* Scapin, I can't take any more.

SCAPIN Oh, monsieur, you should have seen what he did to me. He broke my back.

GERONTE Yours? He broke mine!

SCAPIN No, no, he hit me, me.

GERONTE Me, me. I felt the blows. I can still feel them.

SCAPIN But I'm raw, bleeding. Maybe he caught you with the end of the stick.

GERONTE You should have moved well away from the sack, for my sake.

SCAPIN *(Pushing Géronte's head down again)* Watch it! Here's another of them. He looks even more fierce. *(He imitates approaching footsteps.)*
Gott in Himmel, all de day I run around like a crezzy mann und I no dis Cheront find can.
—*(To Géronte)* Stay down, monsieur.
—Herr Man, I for dis Cheront look. You can me where he is tell?
—No, monsieur, I have no idea where Géronte could be.
—I heff for him a liddle someding. Zvelf gut crecks on de beck mit mein schtick und a few nize sword drusts troo de gotts.
—I'm sorry, monsieur, I can't help you.
—I dink I in dis seck sommding moof see.
—I beg your pardon, monsieur.
—Ja, sommding in dere fonny goes on.
—Couldn't possibly be.
—I dry push troo de seck mein sword.
—No, monsieur, please don't do that.
—You led me vut ist in der seck look ett.
—I don't think so.
—You not dink so?
—You have no right to look in there. This is a private sack.
—I vill in dere look.
—You will not.
—You dink you ken me schtop?
—These are only some old clothes of mine.
—Led me dem see.
—I refuse.
—Ha, refusen, ja?
—That's right.
—Und vut if I on der beck mit mein schtick bead you?
—You'd better not.
—You choking mit me?
—Oh, ow, no, ow, stop it, monsieur, ow!
—You heff now a leedle lesson gelernt, nein? Not to me der beck talk zu giff. Auf wiedersehen.

(He imitates retreating footsteps.) Rotten babbling illiterate! Oh, oh!

GERONTE *(Emerging from the sack)* I'm a wreck.

SCAPIN I'm a corpse.

GERONTE What have they got against my poor old back?

SCAPIN *(Pushing his head down)* Look out, this time there's a gang of them, soldiers. *(He imitates many footsteps and a variety of voices.)* Spread out, men, cover every inch of this neighborhood, and then comb through the whole town. / Stop at every house. / Ask every person. / Search every room, every corner. / Which way now? / Over here? / No, there. /You go right, you others left.
(Whispering to Géronte) Stay out of sight!
Hold it, men! /Who's this character? / That's his servant. / Hey, fellow, where did your master run off to?
—Please, gentlemen, don't hit me!
—Then tell us where he is. / Quick, now, no shuffling, no arguments!
—Gentlemen, let me catch my breath . . .
(Géronte peers nervously out of the sack and sees what Scapin is up to.)
—See these clubs? Tell us where he is right away or we'll drown you in blood.
—I'll suffer any punishment sooner than betray my master.
—We'll smash your head in.
—Do your worst.
—You really want us to?
—I won't rat on my master.
—Give him a taste, boys! / There!
—Oh, dear God!
He raises his stick, sees Géronte standing in front of him, and scoots off.

GERONTE Why, that treacherous, hateful, spiteful liar! He wanted to murder me! *(He staggers out of the sack.)*

Enter Zerbinette.

ZERBINETTE *(Smiling, without seeing Géronte)* That broke me up. I need a breath of air.

GERONTE   *(Aside, without seeing Zerbinette)*   I swear you'll pay for this.

ZERBINETTE   *(Laughing helplessly)*   A great story! What a dunce that old man must be!

GERONTE   Is it so amusing? Who gave you the right to laugh?

ZERBINETTE   Who, me? What do you mean, monsieur?

GERONTE   You have no business laughing at me.

ZERBINETTE   At you?

GERONTE   Of course, me.

ZERBINETTE   Why should I laugh at you?

GERONTE   And to my face!

ZERBINETTE   This has nothing to do with you. Somebody just told me the most hilarious story, which I'm still enjoying, maybe because I have a personal stake in it. So funny! A young man tricked his father out of some money.

GERONTE   A young man did that? To his own father? For money?

ZERBINETTE   He certainly did. Wouldn't you like to know how? I'm itching to tell somebody.

GERONTE   Please do. I'm itching to hear it.

ZERBINETTE   My pleasure. It won't hurt if I repeat it, because it's bound to come out soon. I was recently traveling with a band of Romanies, those people we call gypsies, from one place to the next, telling fortunes and so forth. When we stopped off at this city, a young man saw me, fell smack in love, and started following me around. At first he thought, like any young man, that all he had to do was say the word, and I'd be his. But he soon had second thoughts — I'm not that easy. He told the Romanies, and they said they'd let me go, but for money. Of course, when it came to money, like most well-dressed young men he was naked. His father, who's wealthy, happens to be the king of the skinflints.

Wait. Why can't I remember his name? Can you help me out?
Who has the tightest fist in this city, do you know?

GERONTE No.

ZERBINETTE Something to do with *ron* or *ronte*. Yes, Oronte.
No, Géronte. That's it, Géronte! He's my miser, the tightwad I
was referring to. So anyway, the Romanies planned to leave the
city today and my beau, who still didn't have a penny to scratch
himself with, would have lost me if it hadn't been for his clever
servant. The servant's name I do remember. It's Scapin, and he's a
marvel. I couldn't praise him too highly.

GERONTE *(Aside)* Oh you scheming, thieving . . .

ZERBINETTE And this is how he put one over on the old meanie.
(She laughs raucously.) Every time I think of it I can't stop
laughing. *(More laughter.)* He told the old — ha ha ha ha ha ha —
the old grasper that while he was taking a stroll near the harbor with
the young man — they saw a —ha ha ha ha ha — saw this Turkish
galley and went on board, and this young Turk gave them a — ha ha
ha ha — a nice meal and while they were eating, the galley pulled
away from the shore and the Turk sent back the servant to say he
was taking the son to Algiers if he didn't come up with five hundred
— ha ha ha ha — crowns. Can't you picture the old money-grubber
now? Tormented! His affection for his son battles with his passion
for his gold! To him five hundred crowns are five hundred — ha ha
ha ha — stab wounds. He can't give up that much; it's major
surgery. The pain he'll suffer. He thinks feverishly of any other
way to get his — ha ha ha ha —son back. He wants to prosecute
the — ha ha ha — Turkish galley. He asks the servant to take his
son's place while he scratches up the money he doesn't — ha ha ha
ha — intend to give. To raise the five hundred crowns he'll sell
four or five old suits that are not — ha ha ha — worth twenty. Each
time he comes up with a fresh proposal, the servant explains how
senseless it is and hears the same old refrain: "Why the hell did he
have to go aboard that galley? That goddam galley! That
contemptible, diabolical Turk!" So, after holding out the money and
refusing to let go of it, after sighs and groans galore, he — But you
don't seem to find the story entertaining. What do you say to it?

GERONTE I say the young man ought to be hanged and he'll be
unmercifully punished by his father. I say the gypsy girl is tactless
and insolent to glory in the misfortunes of an honorable man, and

she'll soon get what she deserves for seducing innocent youngsters. As for the servant — that servant, that felon! — by this evening Géronte will put his neck where it belongs — in a noose. *(Exit, fuming.)*

Enter Silvestre.

SILVESTRE What are you doing out here? Don't you know that man you were talking to is your sweetheart's father?

ZERBINETTE I just realized it. And I told him that story about himself.

SILVESTRE Story?

ZERBINETTE I heard it a few minutes ago and I was bursting to tell it again. Too bad for him. Who cares? For us it won't make matters better or worse.

SILVESTRE You had to wag your big tongue. Can't keep private affairs to yourself.

ZERBINETTE He'd have heard it from someone else, wouldn't he?

ARGANTE'S VOICE Silvestre!

SILVESTRE *(To Zerbinette)* Go back inside. That's my master calling.

Exit Zerbinette. Enter Argante.

ARGANTE So you've been plotting, have you? You and Scapin and my son in cahoots? To swindle me! You think I'll stand for that?

SILVESTRE If Scapin has swindled you, monsieur, it's nothing to do with me. I wash my hands of him.

ARGANTE We'll see, you faker, we'll see about that. Nobody puts one over on me and gets away with it.

Enter Géronte.

GERONTE Oh, Argante, I've been skinned. I'm heartsick.

ARGANTE   So am I.

GERONTE   That Scapin tricked me out of five hundred crowns.

ARGANTE   And me out of two hundred francs.

GERONTE   As if five hundred crowns were not enough, he abused me in a way I'm ashamed to mention. But I'll show him.

ARGANTE   So will I for what he did to me.

GERONTE   Will I ever make an example of him!

SILVESTRE   *(Aside)*   I only pray they leave me out of this!

GERONTE   But there's more, Argante. A second misfortune always rides on the back of the first. I was looking forward to having my daughter with me again today. I was so proud of her. Now I learn that she left Taranto long ago and her ship must have gone down at sea.

ARGANTE   Why did you let her stay in Taranto, and not here, in your care?

GERONTE   I had my reasons, family interests, which compelled me to keep my second marriage a close secret. But . . . can it be. . .? *(Enter Nérine.)* Her nurse, Nérine!

NERINE   Oh, Signor Pandolphe, may I —

GERONTE   Don't use that name. I adopted it while I was with you in Taranto. I don't need it any longer. I am called Géronte.

NERINE   So that's it? No wonder we had so much aggravation trying to find you under the other name!

GERONTE   What happened to my daughter and my wife?

NERINE   Your daughter is nearby, monsieur. Before I take you to her, I must ask you to forgive me. I allowed her to marry. We didn't know if we'd ever see you again.

GERONTE   She's married!

NERINE   Yes, monsieur.

GERONTE   To whom?

NERINE   A young man named Octave. He's the son of a certain Argante.

GERONTE   Oh my God!

ARGANTE   What a fluke! An unbelievable coincidence!

GERONTE   Take us, take us to her!

NERINE   This is the house. Step inside.

GERONTE   After you. Come, Argante, come!

The three of them troop into the house.

SILVESTRE   *(Alone)* One surprise after another!

Enter Scapin.

SCAPIN   Hello, Silvestre. What are our people up to?

SILVESTRE   I have two bits of news for you. First, Octave's marriage is cleared up — it turns out that our Hyacinte is Géronte's daughter. Chance took over and completed the elaborate plans of the fathers. Second, the two old men, and especially Géronte, swear they'll have your hide.

SCAPIN   Pooh. Threats have never done me harm. They sail past, 'way overhead, like clouds.

SILVESTRE   You be careful. The sons could easily make up with their fathers and leave you hanging.

SCAPIN   Let me handle it. I'll find a way to cool them off.

SILVESTRE   Get going. They're coming out.

Exit Scapin. Enter Géronte, Argante, Nérine, and Hyacinte.

GERONTE   Come, dear, we'll go to my house. My happiness would have been complete if I'd seen your mother again.

ARGANTE   And here's Octave. Perfect timing. *(Enter Octave.)* Come, my boy, join us in celebrating your marriage. By chance —

OCTAVE   *(Not seeing Hyacinte)*   No, father, I can't go along with your plans. No more deception. You've heard that I'm already spoken for.

ARGANTE   Yes, but you don't know —

OCTAVE   I know everything I need to know.

ARGANTE   I mean that Géronte's daughter —

OCTAVE   His daughter can never be anything to me.

ARGANTE   She's the very —

OCTAVE   No, father. I'm sorry. I've made up my mind.

SILVESTRE   Will you listen?

OCTAVE   I will not. And you shut up.

ARGANTE   Your wife —

OCTAVE   I said no, father. I'll die sooner than give up my lovely Hyacinte. *(He crosses to her.)*   Here she is, and I don't care what you do; I'm pledged to her, and I'll love her as long as I live. I will not marry any other woman.

ARGANTE   For God's sake! She's the woman I'm giving you. What a donkey! He takes a position and won't budge.

HYACINTE   Yes, darling. Monsieur Géronte is my father. Our troubles are over.

GERONTE   Come with me. We can talk more comfortably at home.

Enter Zerbinette.

HYACINTE   Father, I want you to meet a dear friend of mine. When you get to know her you'll be as fond of her as I am.

GERONTE   You want me to make friends with a woman your brother's infatuated with, after she deliberately insulted me?

ZERBINETTE   Forgive me, monsieur. I'd never have said such things if I'd realized who you were. I knew of you only by reputation.

GERONTE   What reputation?

HYACINTE   Father dear, Léandre does love her sincerely. She's a good person, I assure you.

GERONTE   What next? Now they want me to marry my son to a nobody, a tramp.

Enter Léandre.

LEANDRE   Father, you can't fret that the girl I love is penniless and from an unknown background. The gypsies I ransomed her from have just told me she belonged originally to a decent family in this city. They stole her when she was four. She wore this bracelet. It may help us trace her parents.

ARGANTE   If this is her bracelet, she's my long-lost daughter! She disappeared when she was four years old.

GERONTE   Not your daughter?

ARGANTE   Yes. When I look at her I can see the resemblance. Same features exactly.

HYACINTE   One surprise after another!

Enter Carle.

CARLE   Ladies and gentlemen, there's been a strange accident.

GERONTE   What?

CARLE   Poor Scapin. . .

GERONTE   That twister! I'll string him up.

CARLE   Unfortunately, monsieur, you won't have to bother. As he walked past a building a mason's hammer fell on him, cracked his skull, and exposed the brains. He's dying. He begs you to let him say a few words before the end.

ARGANTE   One surprise after another! Where is he?

CARLE   Here.

Enter Scapin, supported by two men, his head heavily bandaged.

SCAPIN   Oh, my friends, as you see . . . Oh, as you see, I'm in a bad way. Oh! I can't die until I speak to all those I've offended: forgive me. Aiee! Before I breathe my last, I apologize from the bottom of my heart for whatever I may have done, and most of all to Monsieur Argante and Monsieur Géronte.

ARGANTE   I forgive you. May you die in peace.

SCAPIN   And you, monsieur, you're the one I injured the most with that beating. . .

GERONTE   I forgive you too. Say no more.

SCAPIN   It was cruel of me to keep on beating you, and —

GERONTE   Let it go at that.

SCAPIN   In my final moments, I'm tormented by that wicked beating —

GERONTE   Almighty God, enough!

SCAPIN   Blow after blow after pitiless blow —

GERONTE   Will you stop! I've forgotten it already.

SCAPIN   Ah, the kindness of this man! He genuinely forgives me, don't you, monsieur, for every one of those blows that —

GERONTE   Yes, yes, yes! Not one more word. I forgive you completely.

SCAPIN   Ah, now I feel much better.

GERONTE   Do you?   But I forgive you only if you die.

SCAPIN   What was that, monsieur?

GERONTE   If you recover, I retract.

SCAPIN   Aiee, aiee!   I feel worse again.

ARGANTE   Make it a perfect day, Géronte.   Give him an absolute pardon, no strings attached.

GERONTE   Agreed.

ARGANTE   Come in to supper, all of you.   We'll share the taste of our joys.

SCAPIN   Carry me to the head of the table and see how long it takes me to die.

The end of

The Scams of Scapin

DON JUAN
or, A Statue to Supper

(Dom Juan, ou le Festin de pierre)

Don Juan
Sganarelle, his valet
Elvire, his wife
Gusman, Elvire's equerry
Don Carlos, Elvire's brother
Don Alonse, another brother of Elvire
Don Louis, Don Juan's father
A Poor Man
Charlotte, a peasant girl
Mathurine, another peasant girl
Pierrot, a peasant
Statue of the Commander
La Violette, Don Juan's lackey
Ragotin, another of Don Juan's lackeys
Monsieur Dimanche, a merchant
La Ramée, a roughneck
Servants of Don Juan, Don Carlos, and Don Alonse
A Specter

The play takes place in Sicily.

ACT ONE

Sganarelle and Gusman in a downstairs room of a palace.

SGANARELLE *(Holding a snuff box)* Whatever Aristotle and the rest of the philosophers say, there's nothing finer than a sniff of snuff. The best people have a passion for it; and anyone who lives without it doesn't deserve to live. Snuff not only cheers and clears your brain, but also improves your soul. You become high-minded; you learn to act like a gentleman. Watch someone take a pinch: he immediately turns friendly, loves to pass the box around, right and left, no matter where he is. He doesn't even wait for the others to ask him; he's ahead of their wishes. That proves how snuff inspires people who take it, makes them kind and honest. Enough of that. Let's go back to our discussion. You say the mistress was shocked when we took off? She came chasing after us because she loves the master so much she can't go on without him? You know what I think? Between us, I'm afraid her love's an investment with a rotten return. There's no real point in Doña Elvire's trip here. You might as well have stayed put.

GUSMAN Why? Tell me straight, Sganarelle, please. What's behind that depressing remark? Did your master confide in you and say he had to leave because he now feels cool toward us?

SGANARELLE No, but that's how it looks to me. He hasn't spoken one word about it, but I'll bet I'm right. I could be wrong, but I've already seen plenty — enough to make things clear to me.

GUSMAN What? He ran off all of a sudden because he's unfaithful to that pure, loving lady? How could he?

SGANARELLE You see, he's still young and doesn't have the heart —

GUSMAN Could a man of honor act so sneakily?

SGANARELLE Honor? Some handicap that is! As if honor would hold him back. . .

GUSMAN   But the holy bonds of matrimony and . . . so forth?

SGANARELLE   Oh, my poor Gusman, my friend, you still don't realize what sort of man Don Juan is.

GUSMAN   True, that I can't imagine, if he has been treacherous. But after he professed so much love and impatience, choked up on so many compliments and vows, sighed, wept, wrote passionate notes and declarations, swore oath after oath, went into ecstasies, raptures, and finally broke into the convent to snatch Doña Elvire away— no, after all that, I certainly don't understand how he could have the heart to go back on his promises.

SGANARELLE   Me, I have little trouble understanding it, and if you knew this individual, you'd see it's easy enough for him. I don't say his feelings for Doña Elvire have changed; I'm still not sure. As you know, he ordered me to go ahead, and since he got here he hasn't mentioned it to me. But let me inform you in confidence that Don Juan is the most shameless sinner ever born, a madman, a demon, a brute, a heretic. He doesn't believe in heaven, hell, or werewolves. He lives like a wild beast, like an Epicurean pig — as debauched as Sardanapalus. He shuts his ears to all reproaches; mocks everything people like us believe in. You say he married your mistress: so what? To glut his passion he'd go on to marry you, her dog and her cat. A marriage costs him nothing; it's his usual way of trapping beauties. He'll marry them all. Older women, younger women, middle-class or peasants — they're never too hot or too cold for his taste. If I told you all the women he's married in different places, I'd be reciting the list till this evening. Gusman, suddenly you've gone pale. But this is no more than a sketch of his personality To fill in the details of the portrait would take a lot more brushwork. Some day the wrath of heaven will come down on him. I'd much sooner work for the Devil. He makes me witness so many horrors that I wish him somewhere else. But a wicked nobleman is a frightening master. I must remain loyal to him, in spite of myself. My fear drives out my natural enthusiasm; it holds my feelings in check and often reduces me to praising what I detest. He's coming now to explore the palace. Let's not stay together. Listen, though: I've spoken frankly and maybe a little too fast. If anything that came out of my mouth reaches his ears I'll call you a liar.

Exit Gusman. Enter Don Juan.

DON JUAN   Who was that talking to you? It looked like Doña Elvire's servant, Gusman.

SGANARELLE   Just about.

DON JUAN   It was?

SGANARELLE   The very man.

DON JUAN   He's been in town since when?

SGANARELLE   Yesterday evening.

DON JUAN   For what purpose?

SGANARELLE   You can guess why he's upset.

DON JUAN   No doubt because we left.

SGANARELLE   He's mortified, poor man. Wanted me to give him the reason.

DON JUAN   What did you answer?

SGANARELLE   I said you hadn't told me.

DON JUAN   But what do you think? What do you make of this business?

SGANARELLE   Me? With all respect, I think you're thinking of some new love affair.

DON JUAN   That's what you think?

SGANARELLE   Yes.

DON JUAN   You're not wrong. I confess: someone else has pushed Elvire out of my thoughts.

SGANARELLE   Well, good God, I know my Don Juan down to his fingertips. I also know your heart's the greatest runner of all time; it enjoys trotting from one liaison to the next — doesn't like to get stuck in one spot.

DON JUAN   And what do you make of that? Am I right?

SGANARELLE   Well, master . . .

DON JUAN   What? Out with it!

SGANARELLE   Of course you're right, if that's what you want. I can't argue there. But if it's not what you want, that's something else again.

DON JUAN   No, speak freely. You have my permission. What's your opinion?

SGANARELLE   In that case, master, I tell you candidly that I don't approve of your ways. Not at all. I consider it downright ah, naughty to sprinkle your love in every direction.

DON JUAN   Do you expect a man to remain the property of the first object that catches him? To give up the world for it? Never to look at anything again? A great idea — to take pride in false morality, to remain forever faithful, shrouded in one passion, with our eyes dead from youth onward to all those beauties elsewhere. No, no: constancy is for corpses. All lovely women deserve the chance to charm us. Because one of them was lucky enough to be the first we met, she has no right to rob the rest of their share of love. I delight in beauty everywhere I find it. I gladly give in to that delicious violence that drags us in its wake. I may utter a pledge, but my love for one beauty doesn't pledge me to be unfair to the others. I keep my eyes open to the fascinations of them all, and confer on each one the most suitable, natural compliments and tributes. I can't withhold my love from everything I find lovable. What happens later — happens. A beautiful face has only to ask for my heart. If I had ten thousand hearts, I'd give them all. There is something indescribable and thrilling in a fresh affair. The entire pleasure of love lies in how it changes. We gradually win over the heart of a young beauty. We see ourselves advancing day by day as we attack her with our adulation and raptures, our tears and sighs pitted against the innocent modesty of an untested soul. We press forward against her petty rebuffs and overcome the scruples she feels she must respect. And at last we gently lead her where we want her to arrive. What a sweet accomplishment! But once we've mastered her, what's left to wish for? Passion is over. Beauty has turned stale. We lull ourselves to sleep unless some new object awakens our desires and holds out the challenge of a fresh conquest. In the end, nothing is more exhilarating than wearing down the resistance of a beautiful woman. In this respect I'm like those empire-builders who flit from victory to victory: the only thing they can't conquer is their ambition. I allow no obstacle to stand in the way of my explosive desires. I have a heart large enough to yearn for the whole earth, and like Alexander, I could wish for other worlds to conquer, but with love.

SGANARELLE   My sainted soul, you can talk! As if you'd learned that by heart. As if you read it from a book.

DON JUAN   And what do you say to it?

SGANARELLE   Good heavens, I say that . . . I don't know what to say. You twist things so that you sound right; yet you're not. I had some clever thoughts ready but that talk of yours has mixed them all up. Let it go for now: I'll write my arguments down; then we'll debate.

DON JUAN   Good.

SGANARELLE   But do I still have your permission to speak freely, master, if I say I'm sort of shocked at the life you lead?

DON JUAN   Oh? What life *do* I lead?

SGANARELLE   A great life. Still, when I see you remarry once a month —

DON JUAN   What could be more enjoyable?

SGANARELLE   All right, I'll admit it's most enjoyable and entertaining. I could go for it myself if it wasn't wrong. But fooling around like this, master, with holy wedlock, and —

DON JUAN   That's between God and me. He and I will sort it out. You don't need to bother about it.

SGANARELLE   I always heard that it's wicked to take the Lord's name in vain, and that freethinkers never come to a good end.

DON JUAN   Haven't I told you enough times, you dunderhead, that I don't like being admonished?

SGANARELLE   I don't mean you, God forbid. You know what you're doing. You have your reasons for being an unbeliever. But there are others, little men who put on a big front, freethinkers who don't know why; they think it suits them. Now if I had a master like that I'd look him straight in the face and say, "How dare you make fun of God! Aren't you scared to mock the holiest things? Who gave you the right, you worm, you louse" — I'm speaking to this other master — "the right to ridicule what everyone else worships? Do you think, because you're a master and wear a frizzy white wig and feathers in your hat and a jacket with gold trimmings and ribbons the color of flames —" I'm not talking to you but to him — "do you think all that makes you smarter, so you can say and do what you please, and nobody will tell you where you get off? I may be your servant, but let me inform you that sooner or later God punishes atheists, and a wicked life will mean a wicked death, and —"

DON JUAN   Stop!

SGANARELLE   Why? What is it?

DON JUAN   "It" is a beautiful girl I'm in love with. I was so attracted I followed her all the way here.

SGANARELLE   But this is where you killed the Commander only six months ago. Aren't you nervous?

DON JUAN   Why? Didn't I do it fairly?

SGANARELLE   Very fairly. Yes, very fully. He can't complain.

DON JUAN   And they pardoned me.

SGANARELLE   Yes, officially, but what about his relatives and friends?

DON JUAN   Let's not think about the unpleasant things that could happen, only about the pleasure of this moment. The girl I mentioned is engaged, the loveliest thing you ever saw. Her fiancé has just escorted her here. By chance I caught sight of them three or four days before they left. Never have I seen two people so happy with each other. They radiated love. And aroused the same emotion in me. I was struck to the heart: it all began with jealousy. I couldn't stand seeing them so much in love. My desire was multiplied by spite. I thought about the joy it would give me to break up this tender arrangement, which jarred my sensibilities. But all my efforts so far have proved useless. I have one last remedy. Today he is treating her to a boat trip out to sea. I didn't tell you before, but I've made all the plans for consummating my love. With a little boat and some men I've hired, I intend to make off with her.

SGANARELLE Ah but, master —

DON JUAN Well?

SGANARELLE You're doing the right thing in the right way. I always say, when you want something badly, go for it.

DON JUAN Get yourself ready. You're coming with me. Make sure you bring all my weapons, so that — *(He notices Doña Elvire approaching.)* Elvire! That's infuriating. You dog! You didn't tell me she was here.

SGANARELLE You didn't ask.

DON JUAN Is she mad to travel to the city without changing her country clothes?

Enter Doña Elvire.

DONA ELVIRE Won't you be gracious enough, Don Juan, to acknowledge me? May I at least hope you'll turn your head in this direction?

DON JUAN I admit I'm surprised, madame. I didn't expect you here.

DONA ELVIRE So I see. You *are* surprised, but not in the way I was hoping for. Your reception confirms what I kept refusing to believe. I marvel at my innocence and soft heart. I would not face up to this betrayal when it was obvious to me. I was easygoing enough, or rather, silly enough, to deceive myself willingly as I fought against my eyes and my judgment. I found excuses for your declining affection; dreamed up a hundred reasons why you might have rushed away; defended you against the charge leveled by my commonsense. Day after day I brushed aside my suspicions, ignoring the voice in me that pronounced you guilty. I reassured myself by listening, instead, to my fantasies, my ridiculous yearnings, for I still *wanted* to believe you faithful. But your greeting just now destroys my remaining hopes. The look you gave me tells me much more than I wish to know. And yet I'd be glad to hear the reasons from your own mouth for your departure. Please, Don Juan, speak. How will you justify your behavior?

DON JUAN Here's Sganarelle, madame. He knows my reasons.

SGANARELLE *(Aside, to Don Juan)* Please, master! I don't know a thing.

DONA ELVIRE Well? Speak up, Sganarelle. I don't care which one of you tells me.

DON JUAN *(Beckoning Sganarelle forward)* Go on. Tell her.

SGANARELLE *(Aside, to Don Juan)* What do you want me to say?

DONA ELVIRE Come closer, if that's what he wants, and let me know why you went off so abruptly.

DON JUAN You won't answer?

SGANARELLE *(Aside, to Don Juan)* I have no answer. Master, you're playing games with me.

DON JUAN Answer her, I tell you.

SGANARELLE Madame . . .

DONA ELVIRE Yes?

SGANARELLE *(Turning back to his master)* Monsieur . . .

DON JUAN *(Threateningly)* If you don't —

SGANARELLE Madame, the reasons why we left are the empire-builders, Alexander, and the other worlds. There, master, that's all I can say.

DONA ELVIRE Don Juan, would you care to shed light on these mysteries?

DON JUAN To tell you the truth, madame . . .

DONA ELVIRE Well, what a weak defense you offer for a courtier, a man to whom this must be a routine matter! You're all confused. I pity you. Why not brazen it out? Put on a lofty front. Swear your feelings for me haven't changed. You still love me with unequaled warmth. Only death can separate us. Say the most urgent business compelled you to leave without letting me know. If you are detained here for a while, against your own wishes, all I have to do is return home and you'll follow me as soon as you can. You ache to be back with me because as long as we're apart you suffer the torture of a body deprived of its soul. Defending yourself like that is much better than stumbling over your words.

DON JUAN I own, madame, that I lack the ability to dissemble. I have a sincere heart. I certainly won't say my feelings for you haven't changed or that I ache to be back with you. By now it's evident that I ran away from you — not for the reasons you perhaps imagine, but out of conscience. I realized I could not go on living with you in sin. My better feelings returned. My inner eyes opened and revealed what I was doing. I was stricken to think I had married you after stealing you from the confines of a cloister; that you'd broken your holy vows, your first commitment; and that God frowns jealously on such actions. Repentance overcame me; I was afraid of His anger. I saw our marriage as no more than adultery in disguise, which invited a penalty from on high. Therefore, I must forget you and allow you the opportunity to return to your prior attachment. Do you oppose this pious resolve, madame? Shall I keep you and invoke God's revenge? Or —

DONA ELVIRE Oh, you wretch, now I know you through and through! It's unfortunately too late — the knowledge only sends me into despair. But you won't escape the punishment you deserve from the very God you mock.

DON JUAN Hear that, Sganarelle? God!

SGANARELLE Yes, we don't set much store by that, do we?

DON JUAN Madame —

DONA ELVIRE Enough. I don't wish to hear any more. I should have stopped listening before this. It's a disgrace to air my shame at more length. After the first word an honest soul ought to know what to do. Never fear: I won't break into names and reproaches. Oh no. I won't waste my anger on words; I'm saving it for my revenge. I repeat that God will punish you for your wickedness; and if the thought of God doesn't frighten you, then beware of the fury of an insulted woman. *(Exit.)*

SGANARELLE *(Aside)* Maybe he finally feels sorry.

DON JUAN *(After reflecting)* Let's consider how to put our boating plan into action.

SGANARELLE Oh, what an abominable master!

ACT TWO

A sea-shore. Charlotte and Pierrot.

CHARLOTTE   Good for you, Pierrot. You got to them just in time.

PIERROT   I'll say. Close to being drowned they was, the both of 'em.

CHARLOTTE   Must have been that storm this morning that turned 'em over.

PIERROT   Yeh. Listen, Charlotte, I'll tell you the whole story, the God so help me truth. I seen 'em first; seen 'em first, I did. Me and fat Lucas was kidding around on the beach, throwing sand in each other's eyes, just for kicks. You know fat Lucas: he likes his fun, and me too, I need my kicks once in a while. So there we was, fistfuls of sand flying, when I noticed something 'way out there in the waves jiggling around like it was bobbing toward us. I keep my eyeballs fixated on it till suddenly I see I can't see it.
      So I go, "Hey, Lucas, see them men out there swimming?"
      And he goes, "Come off it, you must have watched a cat die and that give you a squint."
      So I go, "Fooey on you, my eyes're as unsquinty as yours. Couple of men, I tell you."
      And he goes, "Not a prayer — you're cross-eyed."
      So I go, "You want to bet? I'm no cross-eyes. Two men — look at 'em — swimming clear this way."
      And he goes, "Crap, I'll bet they never are."
      So I go, "You want to lay ten on it?"
      And he goes, "Sure do . . . here's my money down."
      Me, I'm nobody's fool, Charlotte, not even a halfwit. Bold as you like, I slap down my singles and halfs and quarters, quicker than you could chugalug a glass of wine, because me, I'm a betting man and when I go, I go the limit. But this time it wasn't no risk. I'm nobody's sucker. Sure enough, soon as we laid the bet, I could see the men again, plain as Lucas' belly, waving to us for help. So I pick up the whole pot and I go, "Lucas, you see 'em now, they're yelling. Let's go save 'em."
      So he goes, "Not me. They made me lose."

Well, to cut the story off at the edges, I, you know, lecturize him till he jumps in the boat with me. Out at sea we wrestle and struggle, hup, ho, and drag the both of 'em out of the water and take 'em home to a big fire and they sit and dry off in the raw buff. Later two more of 'em shows up because they rescued themselves out of the water. Next, Mathurine walks in and one of 'em gives her the eye. So that's it, Charlotte, the whole story.

CHARLOTTE But Pierrot, didn't you tell me one of 'em's nicer-looking than the rest?

PIERROT Ah, the master. He's got to be some big, big nobleman, because of the gold all the way up and down his jacket. His servants are kind of noble, too. Still and all, big-big or not so big, he was a goner if we didn't reached him just in time. Soaked to the gills and suffocuted, he was.

CHARLOTTE Come off it. . .

PIERROT No exaggication. By now he'd be some shark's dinner.

CHARLOTTE Is he still in the raw buff?

PIERROT Nah, they put all his things back on him. We watched. I never saw nothing like how they dressed him up. Yow! These nobles, what a load o' crapdiddle on 'em! Me, I'd lose my way getting into that many clothes. Astoundished I was. They wears hair that comes off their head and stick it back on after they dress like it was one of your bonnets. Their shirt sleeves — Charlotte, you and me could take a stroll inside 'em. No knee-breeches, only a flap of wide stuff. It looks like a apron but it stretches from here to next Easter. No doublet, only a shrimpy little vest down to their plectorals. No collar, only a large scarf like around the neck with tassels hanging down on the belly. On the end of their sleeves they has a sort of collar, and lacy funnels around their knees. And ribbons, Charlotte! strings of ribbons over and under and all moving like a bed of worms. Ribbons on their shoes too, front and back! If I was to take one step in them shoes I'd break my neck.

CHARLOTTE Whoo, Pierrot, I got to see some of this!

PIERROT First listen a sec, Charlotte. Let me tell you something.

CHARLOTTE Yes? What's that then?

PIERROT You see, Charlotte, I must like they say empty out my heart. You know I love you. We're destinated to marry. But Charlotte, you don't satisfy me.

CHARLOTTE How come? What way?

PIERROT Truth is, you decompose my mind.

CHARLOTTE I never do!

PIERROT Yeh, because you don't love me.

CHARLOTTE Ha ha ha. That's all?

PIERROT That's all, but that's enough.

CHARLOTTE My soul, Pierrot, you keep saying the same thing.

PIERROT I keep saying the same thing because it keeps being the same thing, and if it stops being the same thing I'll stop saying the same thing.

CHARLOTTE What am I supposed to do? What do you want?

PIERROT I want you to love me.

CHARLOTTE I don't love you?

PIERROT No, you don't, and yet I try all I can to force you to. I buy you ribbons from every peddler we see. I risk my neck to steal you blackbird eggs. On your birthday I pay that music player to play your favorite tune. But none of that don't do no better than banging my head against a wall. It's unproper, it's unrespectable when folks love us and we don't love 'em back.

CHARLOTTE I do so love you back.

PIERROT Oh sure. Some love that is!

CHARLOTTE What do you want me to do then?

PIERROT Damnation, what we all do when we really love.

CHARLOTTE Don't I really love?

PIERROT   No, or I'd notice it. Folks show they really love other folks from the floor of their heart by teasing 'em. Chubby Thomasine now, she's out of her skull for young Robin; hangs around him all day, annoys him, won't give him a second to hisself, always up to some game with him . . . whaps him on the head every time she goes past him. Or, like the other day, he's sitting on a stool and she tugs it out from under him and he sprawls in the mud. That's real love.   But you, you don't never speak a word to me; you sit like a block of wood. If I walk past you twenty times you won't budge, no, not to wallop me one or swear at me or nothing. That's no good, Charlotte. You're too frigidified.

CHARLOTTE   What can I do about it? That's my personality. I can't be the same's other folks.

PIERROT   This isn't nothing to do with personality. When you have a liking for people you give 'em a sign.

CHARLOTTE   Well, I like you as much as I can. If that's not enough, go love someone else.

PIERROT   See what I mean? If you did love me, would you ever say a thing like that?

CHARLOTTE   How come you keep naggling at me about this?

PIERROT   It wouldn't hurt you, would it, what I'm asking for? Couldn't you be a bit more friendly?

CHARLOTTE   Oh, give it a rest. Then maybe all of a sudden, without thinking about it, it'll happen.

PIERROT   Let's shake on that, Charlotte.

CHARLOTTE   Well . . . all right.

PIERROT   And promise you'll try to love me more.

CHARLOTTE   I'll do what I can, but it'll have to come on its own . . . Pierrot, is that the nobleman?

PIERROT   Yes, he's the one.

CHARLOTTE   Isn't he pretty! What a shame if he'd went under!

PIERROT See you soon. I'm pooped. Must down a beer or two and reciprocate some of my energy. *(Exit.)*

Enter Don Juan and Sganarelle.

DON JUAN We lost out there, Sganarelle. The storm overturned not only our boat but also our plan. Still, meeting that peasant girl — and what a charmer she is! — offsets our bad luck. I can't let her get away. I've already dropped some hints. She won't keep me waiting and sighing for long.

SGANARELLE I must say, master, you amaze me. We barely escaped death, and instead of thanking God for His compassion, you're already trying to stir up His wrath with the same old fantasies of love — *(Don Juan looks threatening.)* Dry up! A lousy servant like you: you have no idea what you're talking about. The master knows what he's up to, doesn't he?

DON JUAN *(Catching sight of Charlotte)* Another peasant girl. Where did she come from, Sganarelle? Did you ever see anything prettier? Isn't she better than the other?

SGANARELLE Definitely. *(Aside)* Another portrait for the gallery. . .

DON JUAN Well, well! Where did you spring from, enchanting young lady? How is it possible that, among these trees and rocks, I suddenly meet a being formed like you?

CHARLOTTE You see what you see, monsieur.

DON JUAN You're from this village?

CHARLOTTE Yes, monsieur.

DON JUAN And you live here?

CHARLOTTE Yes, monsieur.

DON JUAN What's your name?

CHARLOTTE Charlotte. At your service.

DON JUAN You're so lovely! Magnificent eyes!

CHARLOTTE   Monsieur, you make me blush.

DON JUAN   Don't blush to hear the truth. Sganarelle, what do you say? Have you ever come across anything more ravishing? Please, turn around slowly. Ah, a superb figure! Kindly lift your head a bit. Ah, a bewitching face! Open your eyes wide. Magnificent! And just a glimpse of your teeth? Adorable! So are those appetizing lips. I'm overcome. Never have I seen so much charm in one woman.

CHARLOTTE   That's pleasant of you, monsieur, but I hope you're not making fun of me.

DON JUAN   I make fun of you? God forbid! I love you too much, and I say that from the bottom of my heart.

CHARLOTTE   In that case, I'm much obliged.

DON JUAN   Not at all. You're under no obligation to me for what I say. Your beauty has earned it.

CHARLOTTE   You talk too fancy for me, monsieur. I'm not smart — don't know how to reply.

DON JUAN   Sganarelle, take a look at her hands.

CHARLOTTE   Now, now, monsieur. They're black as I don't know what.

DON JUAN   How can you say that? They're the prettiest hands in the world. Let me kiss them, will you?

CHARLOTTE   You're so kind, monsieur. If I'd knew about this before, I'd have cleaned 'em up with bran.

DON JUAN   Tell me then, sweet Charlotte, you're not married, are you?

CHARLOTTE   No, monsieur, but I soon will be, to Pierrot, the son of Simonette, who lives next door.

DON JUAN   What? A woman like you as the wife of some peasant! Never — a wicked waste of all that beauty! You were not born to spend your life in a village. You deserve a much nobler fate. God, who appreciates this, brought me here to put a stop to this marriage and to offer your charms their fitting reward. In other words, I love you, lovely Charlotte, with all my heart. Let me pluck you out of this dismal spot and raise you to the heights you deserve. This love of mine may seem impulsive, but can I help it, when it's the result of your intoxicating beauty? To love as powerfully as I love you after fifteen minutes might, with some other woman, take six months.

CHARLOTTE   Really, monsieur, I don't know what to do when you talk that way. I do like it, and I'd give anything to believe you. But I've always been told a girl can't trust the things gentlemen say to her, especially you people from the court. You tempt us to get your own way with we girls.

DON JUAN   I am not one of those people.

SGANARELLE   *(Aside)*   Not on your life.

CHARLOTTE   Look, monsieur, it's no fun being deceived. I'm a poor country girl, but I'm proud of my good name. I'd sooner see myself dead than dishonored.

DON JUAN   Could I be evil enough to deceive a person of your caliber? Or treacherous enough to dishonor you? Never! I have too strong a conscience. I love you, Charlotte — and I mean honorably. To prove I speak the truth, I swear my only desire is to marry you. Is that sufficient? I'm ready as soon as you say yes. I ask this man here to witness that I will keep my word.

SGANARELLE   Don't worry, girl. He'll marry you all you want.

DON JUAN   Charlotte, I see you don't yet know me. You misjudge me badly when you compare me with others. Perhaps there are some despicable men who try to get what they can from young women, but you mustn't count me among them or doubt my honesty. Besides, your beauty should reassure you. Anyone with your looks is safe from such misgivings. Believe me, everything about you affirms that you are not a woman who *could* be exploited. As for me, if I ever thought, even for a flicker of a second, of deceiving you, I'd put a thousand knives into my heart.

CHARLOTTE   Oh, I'm so befuzzled! I don't know if you're telling the truth, but you make me want to believe you.

DON JUAN   Believe me, believe me! Don't be unfair. Didn't I give you my promise? Will you accept it? Will you be my wife?

CHARLOTTE   Yes. If my aunt lets me.

DON JUAN   Good. You yourself want to, Charlotte, so shake hands on it.

CHARLOTTE   You wouldn't let me down after this, monsieur, would you? That'd be sinful when me, I'm sincere.

DON JUAN   No! You don't still doubt *my* sincerity? Shall I utter some terrible oaths? May God strike —

CHARLOTTE   No, don't swear! I believe you.

DON JUAN   How about a little kiss to seal your word?

CHARLOTTE   Please, monsieur, after we're married. Then I'll give you as many kisses as you want.

DON JUAN   What I want, my sweet Charlotte, is what you want; so let me take your hand and smother it in unending love to express my joy at . . .

Re-enter Pierrot.

PIERROT   *(Bobbing up between them and pushing Don Juan away)* Not so hot, monsieur. Cool off your lungs or you'll catch puresie.

DON JUAN   *(Shoving him back roughly)* Who sent this yokel here?

PIERROT   *(Dodging between Charlotte and Don Juan again)* Keep your distance, I tell you. No handling my sweetheart!

DON JUAN   *(Shoving him aside again)* What is all this bluster?

PIERROT   What's all this shoving folks around?

CHARLOTTE   *(Taking Pierrot's arm)* Pierrot, let him alone.

PIERROT   Let him alone? Not me!

DON JUAN   Ha!

PIERROT   Just 'cause you're some gentleman, you think you can kiss our wives in front of us?   Go kiss your own.

DON JUAN   Hey?

PIERROT   Hey. *(Don Juan slaps him.)*   Watch it!   You better not hit me again. *(Another slap.)*   That does it! *(Another slap.)*   Oh boy! *(Another slap.)*   Dirty devils and horse droppings!   You can't hit people like this.   Some kind of reward, this is, for saving you from going under!

CHARLOTTE   Pierrot, don't lose your temper.

PIERROT   I will lose my temper; and you, you're a slut to let him fondle you.

CHARLOTTE   No, Pierrot, it's not what you think.   The gentleman wants to marry me, so you shouldn't get mad.

PIERROT   What?   When we're engaged?

CHARLOTTE   That doesn't count now, Pierrot.   If you love me, you ought to be happy I'm going to be a lady.

PIERROT   Am I hell!   I'd rather see you dead than somebody else's alive.

CHARLOTTE   Now, now, Pierrot, don't fret.   Once I'm a lady I'll see you do all right out of it.   You can sell us your butter and cheese.

PIERROT   I wouldn't sell you a thing, not if you paid me twice.   A lady!   Is that what he said?   And you listened?   Shoot, if I knew then, I'd never have fished him out of the water.   I'd have bumped him one on the bonko with my oar.

DON JUAN   *(Closing in on Pierrot)*   What did you say?

PIERROT   *(Keeping Charlotte in front of him)*   You don't scare me.

DON JUAN   *(Circling Charlotte)*   Stand still, then.

PIERROT   *(Moving around Charlotte)*   I laugh in your chops.   Ha!

DON JUAN *(Still in pursuit)* We'll see about that.

PIERROT *(Behind Charlotte again)* I know your type.

DON JUAN Yes . . .

SGANARELLE Leave him, master. Poor wretch, it's not fair to hit him. *(To Pierrot, stepping between him and Don Juan)* Listen, lad, take off and don't say another word.

PIERROT *(Passing Sganarelle and confronting Don Juan)* I'll say what I like.

DON JUAN I'll teach you.

He swings at Pierrot, who ducks and stays down. Sganarelle takes the blow.

SGANARELLE *(Looking down at Pierrot)* You goddam idiot.

DON JUAN A reward for your soft heart.

PIERROT I'm going to tell her aunt about all this hoopla. *(Exit.)*

DON JUAN At last I'm going to be the happiest man alive. I wouldn't exchange my luck for all the wealth in the world. What with the pleasure of having you for my wife, and —

Sganarelle notices Mathurine approaching. He lets out a laugh, then corrects it to a warning cough.

MATHURINE *(To Don Juan)* What are you doing there, monsieur, with Charlotte? Are you talking love to her too?

DON JUAN *(Aside, to Mathurine)* No, the reverse. She let me know she'd like to be my wife, and I told her I was engaged to you.

CHARLOTTE What does Mathurine want with you, then?

DON JUAN *(Aside, to Charlotte)* She's jealous. She saw me speaking to you, and wants me to marry her, but I told her I want you.

MATHURINE What? Charlotte —

DON JUAN *(Aside, to Mathurine)* Don't waste your time speaking to her. She's set on this notion.

CHARLOTTE What's all this? Mathurine —

DON JUAN *(Aside, to Charlotte)* She won't listen to you. You can't get this fantasy out of her head.

MATHURINE Does she —?

DON JUAN *(Aside, to Mathurine)* You can't make her see reason.

CHARLOTTE I'd like —

DON JUAN *(Aside, to Charlotte)* She's as stubborn as the devil.

MATHURINE Really —

DON JUAN *(Aside, to Mathurine)* Don't argue with her. She's crazy.

CHARLOTTE I think —

DON JUAN *(Aside, to Charlotte)* Let her be. She's obsessed.

MATHURINE No, no. I must speak to her.

CHARLOTTE I must find out why.

MATHURINE What —?

DON JUAN *(Aside, to Mathurine)* I'll bet she says I promised to marry her.

CHARLOTTE I —

DON JUAN *(Aside, to Charlotte)* What do you bet she insists I said I'd make her my wife?

MATHURINE Hey, Charlotte, it's not fair to cut in on other people.

CHARLOTTE It's not right, Mathurine, to get jealous when this gentleman talks to me.

MATHURINE   He saw me first.

CHARLOTTE   If he saw you first, he saw me second. And promised to marry me.

DON JUAN   *(Aside, to Mathurine)*   Well, what did I say?

MATHURINE   Get out of here. It's me, not you, he promised to marry.

DON JUAN   *(Aside, to Charlotte)*   Didn't I guess?

CHARLOTTE   Please, save that for someone else. It's me, I say.

MATHURINE   Are you joking? It's me.

CHARLOTTE   He'll back me. Ask him if I'm telling a lie.

MATHURINE   If I'm not telling the truth, he won't back me.

CHARLOTTE   Is it true, monsieur? Did you promise to marry her?

DON JUAN   *(Aside, to Charlotte)*   You're making fun of me.

MATHURINE   Is it true, monsieur? Did you swear you'd be her husband?

DON JUAN   *(Aside, to Mathurine)*   How could you think that?

CHARLOTTE   But look, she insists.

DON JUAN   *(Aside, to Charlotte)*   Let her.

MATHURINE   She says it in front of you.

DON JUAN   *(Aside, to Mathurine)*   Let her.

CHARLOTTE   No, no. We must get the truth.

MATHURINE   We must get it straight.

CHARLOTTE   Yes, Mathurine, I want monsieur to show you up.

MATHURINE   Yes, Charlotte, I want monsieur to put you down.

CHARLOTTE   Please, monsieur, settle the argument.

MATHURINE   Yes, monsieur, untangle the whole thing.

CHARLOTTE   *(To Mathurine)*   Now you'll see.

MATHURINE   *(To Charlotte)   You'll*   see.

CHARLOTTE   *(To Don Juan)*   Tell us.

MATHURINE   *(To Don Juan)*   Speak.

DON JUAN   *(Embarrassed, to both of them)*   What do you want me to say? You both contend that I've promised to marry you. Each of you knows how we really stand, don't you, without any further explaining from me? Why make me say it again? The one to whom I actually gave my promise can laugh at the other one. Does she have anything to worry about, so long as I keep that promise? All this talk is getting us nowhere. We must act, not discuss. It's the results that count, not the words. This is the only way I can settle the argument. You'll see, when I marry you, which one I love. *(Aside, to Mathurine)* Let her think what she likes. *(Aside, to Charlotte)* Let her indulge her imagination. *(Aside, to Mathurine)* I adore you. *(Aside, to Charlotte)* I belong to you. *(Aside to Mathurine)* Other faces are ugly compared to yours. *(Aside, to Charlotte)* I look at you and all the others seem repulsive. *(To both)* I have some business to take care of. I'll be back for you in a quarter of an hour. *(Exit.)*

CHARLOTTE   So it's me he loves.

MATHURINE   It's me he'll marry.

SGANARELLE   You poor girls. You're so innocent I feel sorry for you. I hate to see you racing toward disaster. Believe me, both of you: take no notice of the tales you hear. Stay in your village.

DON JUAN   *(As he returns, aside)*   I'd love to know why Sganarelle didn't come with me.

SGANARELLE   My master is a phony. All he wants is to have his way with you, as he's done with so many others. He'd marry the whole human race if — *(Noticing Don Juan)* That's untrue. Whoever told you that, call him a liar. My master would never marry the whole human race. He is not a phony. He does not want to have his way with you, and he has not had his way with others. See, here he is. Ask him.

DON JUAN *(Suspiciously, glaring at Sganarelle)* Yes.

SGANARELLE Master, the world is crowded with slander-mongers. But trust me to beat them back. I was saying that if anyone says an unfavorable word about you, these two mustn't believe it. They must call him a liar.

DON JUAN Sganarelle!

SGANARELLE Yes, my master's a man of honor, that I guarantee.

DON JUAN Hm . . .

SGANARELLE People of that sort are contemptible.

Enter La Ramée.

LA RAMEE *(Aside, to Don Juan)* Monsieur, I must warn you that this is not a healthy spot for you.

DON JUAN Why not?

LA RAMEE A dozen horsemen are looking for you. They should be here any moment. I think I know how they managed to follow you. I heard the news from a peasant. When they questioned him, they described you. It's urgent. The sooner you get away from here, the better. *(Exit.)*

DON JUAN *(To Charlotte and Mathurine)* I'm called away suddenly on business. But I want you to remember my promise. You'll hear from me before tomorrow evening. *(Exeunt Charlotte and Mathurine.)* Twelve against one: I'll need some clever strategy to escape them. I'll have you put on my clothes, Sganarelle, while I —

SGANARELLE Master, don't toy with me. In your clothes I could get killed, and —

DON JUAN Let's move. You should feel honored. It's a lucky servant who has the glory of dying for his master. *(Exit.)*

SGANARELLE Thanks a million for that honor! Please, God, in case it's a matter of life or death, don't let me be taken for anyone else!

.   c

ACT THREE

A forest. Don Juan in country costume, Sganarelle in a doctor's garb.

SGANARELLE Wasn't I right, master? These are marvelous get-ups. Your idea wouldn't have worked. This way we're much better disguised.

DON JUAN Yes, you look fine, though I can't imagine where you unearthed that ridiculous outfit.

SGANARELLE The gown belonged to an old doctor, who had pawned it. I paid out of my own pocket. But you know what, master? People I meet look up to me, bow politely, take me for a learned man, and want to consult me.

DON JUAN For what?

SGANARELLE Five or six peasants so far, men and women — they stopped me and asked about their illnesses.

DON JUAN And you said you had no idea.

SGANARELLE Me? Not a bit. I wanted to uphold the dignity of my gown. I diagnosed each illness and gave out prescriptions.

DON JUAN What remedies did you prescribe?

SGANARELLE Any that occurred to me. Guesswork. If would be a laugh if they were cured and came back to thank me.

DON JUAN Why shouldn't they be cured? Is there any reason for you not to enjoy the same privileges as other doctors? They do no more than you in healing the sick. Their talent is pure invention. They win a reputation on the strength of fluky recoveries, that's all. Like them, you might as well benefit from the patient's luck, and accept the credit for the magic forces of chance and nature.

SGANARELLE   Master, don't tell me you disbelieve in medicine, too?

DON JUAN   It's one of mankind's greatest follies.

SGANARELLE   What? You don't believe in senna pods or cassia or that wine that makes you throw up?

DON JUAN   Why do you expect me to believe in them?

SGANARELLE   You have the soul of an infidel. You know, everybody's talking about that wine lately. Its miracle cures have converted the biggest skeptics. Only three weeks ago I myself saw it in action.

DON JUAN   What happened?

SGANARELLE   A man had been in agony for six days. Nobody knew what to do for him. All the remedies had failed. So finally they gave him the wine.

DON JUAN   And he recovered?

SGANARELLE   No. He died.

DON JUAN   Brilliant result.

SGANARELLE   I'll say. For six days he'd been trying to die. But the wine blanked him out in a second. What could be more effective?

DON JUAN   You're right.

SGANARELLE   But let's move away from medicine, which you don't believe in, and talk about other things, because this gown makes me bold and I feel like disputing with you. Remember, you said I can disagree so long as I don't reproach you.

DON JUAN   Well?

SGANARELLE   I'd like to probe your thoughts. Can it be that you don't believe in God at all?

DON JUAN   Let that go.

SGANARELLE In other words, no. And in hell?

DON JUAN Huh!

SGANARELLE Same again. And in the devil, if you don't mind?

DON JUAN Yes, yes.

SGANARELLE No again. But don't you even believe in the afterlife?

DON JUAN Ha, ha, ha!

SGANARELLE This is one man I'll have a hard time converting.
Tell me now: what do you think of hobgoblins, poltergeists, and
other evil spirits?

DON JUAN You numskull!

SGANARELLE I can't accept that. Nothing's more real than evil
spirits. I'd defend them to the death. A person must have faith in
something. What do you believe?

DON JUAN What I believe?

SGANARELLE Yes.

DON JUAN I believe, Sganarelle, that two and two are four and four
and four are eight.

SGANARELLE That's a belief? Those are articles of faith? From
what I gather, your religion is simple arithmetic. People get strange
ideas in their heads. They study hard and often grow less wise.
Take me, master: I haven't studied the way you have, not a bit,
thank God. Nobody can boast of ever having taught me a thing.
But with my modest share of sense and judgment, I understand
what's what better than all the books. I realize that this world we
see is not a mushroom that sprang up overnight. So let me put it to
you: Who made those trees, these rocks, this earth, and the sky up
there? Did it all create itself? Or you, for instance. There you are
— did you create yourself? Didn't your father have to do something
to your mother? Can you look at all the components of the human
machine without marveling at how they function together — these
nerves, these bones, these veins, these arteries, these . . . this

lung, this heart, this liver, and all these other organs that . . . Blast it! don't you want to interrupt? I can't go on arguing without interruptions. You deliberately say nothing; you let me keep talking out of spite.

DON JUAN I'm waiting for you to clinch your argument.

SGANARELLE My argument is that there's something miraculous in mankind, whatever you say, something all the scholars can't explain. Isn't it a miracle that here I am with a thing in my head that thinks all these different thoughts at once and makes my body do what it commands? I want to clap my hands, raise my arm, lift my eyes to heaven, lower my head, move my feet, go right, go left, forward, back, turn. . . *(While turning, he falls.)*

DON JUAN You broke your argument's nose.

SGANARELLE I'm a prize fool to waste time reasoning with you. Believe what you want: I don't care whether you'll be damned.

DON JUAN During this argument I think we got lost. Call out to that man. Ask him the way.

SGANARELLE Hey there! Hey, fellow! Hey, friend! One word, please.

(Enter a Poor Man.) Where's the road to the town?

THE POOR MAN Keep to this track, gentlemen, and turn right at the edge of the forest. But I advise you to be on guard. For a while now we've had robbers in these parts.

DON JUAN I'm grateful to you, friend. My warmest thanks.

THE POOR MAN Could you help me out, monsieur?

DON JUAN Ha, ha! Your advice, I see, had a selfish motive.

THE POOR MAN I'm poor, monsieur, living alone in this wood for ten years. I'll pray God to give you all kinds of bounty.

DON JUAN Pray for decent clothes for yourself. Don't worry about others.

SGANARELLE My dear man, you don't know this gentleman. All he believes is that two and two are four and four and four are eight.

DON JUAN How do you occupy yourself in this forest?

THE POOR MAN I pray God every day to grant prosperity to the kind people who give me something.

DON JUAN Then you must be quite comfortable.

THE POOR MAN Unfortunately, monsieur, I'm in desperate need.

DON JUAN You're joking. A man who prays all day couldn't be too badly off.

THE POOR MAN Honestly, monsieur, most of the time I don't have a bit of bread to bite into.

DON JUAN Strange. Your good deeds go unrewarded. *(Laughing)* Here: I'll give you a gold coin so long as you utter a blasphemy.

THE POOR MAN Monsieur, you don't expect me to sin?

DON JUAN Never mind that. Do you or don't you want to earn this gold coin? It's yours, as soon as you curse. *(Withdrawing it)* Not yet. Curse!

THE POOR MAN Monsieur . . .

DON JUAN If you don't, you can't have it.

SGANARELLE Go ahead, curse a little. Won't do any harm.

DON JUAN Take it. I'm telling you to take it. After you curse.

THE POOR MAN No, monsieur. I'd rather die hungry.

DON JUAN All right, I give it to you — for the love of humanity. But what's going on there? One man attacked by three? That's cowardly, disgusting — I can't stomach that. *(Exit.)*

SGANARELLE My master's a maniac to risk his life when he doesn't have to. But see, his help turned the trick. The two of them have scared off the other three.

Exit the Poor Man. Enter Don Carlos, sword in hand.

DON CARLOS   You have a mighty arm, monsieur. The flight of
those robbers proves it. I thank you for your courageous
assistance, and —

DON JUAN   *(Reappearing, sword in hand)*   You'd have done the
same in my place, monsieur. Under these circumstances it was a
matter of honor. The cowards! If I hadn't intervened, I'd have
sided with them in effect. How did they happen to catch you?

DON CARLOS   I'd lost my brother and friends. While I was looking
for them, the robbers pounced on me, killed my horse, and without
your selfless efforts, would have done the same to me.

DON JUAN   Are you making for the town?

DON CARLOS   Yes, but not to enter it. My brother and I must keep
to the countryside, thanks to one of those miserable affairs that turn
noblemen and their families into self-sacrificing slaves of honor. At
best, when we're successful, we can only come to a sad end. If we
don't say good-by to life, we must flee into exile and say good-by to
our homeland. That is why I consider a nobleman's lot unfortunate.
Prudent, law-abiding behavior doesn't protect him from the
recklessness of others. His existence, his peace, and his belongings
depend on the whims of the first rash fellow who insults him. To
answer such provocations, an honorable man may have to die.

DON JUAN   There is one compensation in dealing with those who
take it into their heads to offend us: we make them run the same
risks as we do and we give them an equally hard time. Will it be
indiscreet if I inquire about this family affair?

DON CARLOS   There's little sense now in keeping it secret. Once it
becomes known we will not attempt to conceal our shame for mere
reasons of honor. No, let our revenge become equally known,
together with our plan for accomplishing it. And so, monsieur, I
may as well tell you outright that our sister was seduced and
abducted from a convent by a certain Don Juan Tenorio, the son of
Don Louis Tenorio. We have searched for him for several days.
This morning we followed a lead provided by a servant. Don Juan
apparently rode out of town along this coastal route with four or five
companions. But in spite of our careful tracking, we have not found
him.

DON JUAN   Do you know this Don Juan?

DON CARLOS   Not personally. Only from my brother's description and his own ugly reputation. His life has been —

DON JUAN   No more, monsieur, please. He is a sort of friend of mine. It would be ignoble of me to hear him discredited.

DON CARLOS   I won't speak of him further, monsieur, out of gratitude to you. The least I can do after you have saved my life is to refrain in your presence, since you are his acquaintance and I have nothing to say in his favor. But although he is a sort of friend of yours, I hope you do not approve of what he did or find it strange that we are bent on revenge.

DON JUAN   On the contrary, I'd like to help and spare you further trouble. I can't very well prevent myself from being Don Juan's friend, but he should not affront gentlemen without facing the consequences, and I will see that he makes reparation.

DON CARLOS   What reparation can atone for such misdeeds?

DON JUAN   Whatever satisfies your honor. You need not trouble yourself to seek Don Juan further. I will have him appear when and where you wish.

DON CARLOS   That prospect, monsieur, sounds gratifying to one of the injured parties. But after what I owe you, I am distressed to see you on the opposing side.

DON JUAN   I am so close to Don Juan that he could not fight unless I joined him. And so I answer for him as though for myself, and you have only to say when you would like him to appear and make reparation.

DON CARLOS   A cruel coincidence — I owe my life to a friend of Don Juan!

Enter Don Alonse with three followers.

DON ALONSE   *(To his men, not seeing Don Carlos or Don Juan)*
Let the horses drink over there and bring them after us. I'll walk for a while. *(Noticing the others)* What! Can I believe my eyes? My brother with our enemy?

DON CARLOS   Our enemy?

Don Juan steps back three paces and rests his hand on his sword hilt.

DON JUAN   Yes, I am Don Juan. Your advantage in numbers cannot make me renounce my name.

DON ALONSE   *(Drawing his sword)*   Die then for it!

Sganarelle runs for cover.

DON CARLOS   No, brother! I owe him my life. Without his aid I'd have been killed by thieves.

DON ALONSE   Will you let that consideration block our revenge? All the favors we receive from an enemy hand have no power over us. When we compare the debt with the injury, your gratitude seems ridiculous. Honor is infinitely more precious than life. We owe nothing to a man who has saved your life but stolen our honor.

DON CARLOS   I appreciate the distinction a gentleman must always draw between the two. My gratitude does not obliterate my resentment. But let me now repay that life he gave me. I will meet him here in a few days and allow him that much liberty to enjoy the reward for his generous act.

DON ALONSE   No! By putting off our revenge, we may lose it. The chance may never come again. Heaven offers it here and now, and we must make the most of it. We cannot think of pulling back when our honor has suffered so grave a wound. If you find it repugnant to attack him now, stand aside and I'll seize this golden opportunity.

DON CARLOS   Brother, I beg of you —

DON ALONSE   All this useless chatter! He must die.

DON CARLOS   I say again: stop! I swear I will not allow him to be attacked by anyone. I'll defend him to the life, this same life he saved. Before you can reach him with your sword you will have to cut past me.

DON ALONSE   What! You ally yourself with your enemy against your brother? Instead of being enraged like me at the sight of him, you turn soft and sympathetic?

DON CARLOS   We can afford, brother, to be moderate in a just cause, and to avenge our honor without getting carried away, as you are. We can master our hearts, be brave without being savage, and rule our actions with reason, not blind fury. I do not wish to remain indebted to my enemy, and I must, as a priority, settle my obligation to him. Our vengeance will not be compromised because we postpone it; no, it will be more impressive. This opportunity that we have had and chosen to delay will make that vengeance appear more just in the eyes of the world.

DON ALONSE   Oh this strange weakness, this fearful blindness! You jeopardize the demands of our honor with your foolish notion of a debt.

DON CARLOS   No, brother, don't fret. If I am in error, I'll know how to put it right. I accept the responsibility for our honor; I am aware of what it entails. By putting off the day of reckoning for the sake of my gratitude I increase, not quench, my burning desire for satisfaction. Don Juan, you will note that I am careful to requite the gift of life I had from you. You can judge me accordingly. I pay back a debt as warmly as I acknowledge it, and I shall be as exact in responding to your offense as I am to your gift. I am not asking you to explain your intentions now. You are free to decide at your leisure what you must do. You understand how seriously you have affronted us. I leave it to you to determine what compensation is required. Will it be peace or violence and blood? Either will satisfy us. Whichever you choose, you have given your word that I shall receive reparation from Don Juan. Do not forget! Remember also that from now on I am indebted only to my honor.

DON JUAN   I have asked you for nothing. I will live up to my promise.

DON CARLOS   Come, brother. This brief respite will not weaken our resolve.

Exeunt Don Carlos and Don Alonse.

DON JUAN   Hey, Sganarelle!

SGANARELLE *(Coming out of hiding)* Beg your pardon?

DON JUAN Jellyfish! You take off, do you, when I'm in danger?

SGANARELLE Forgive me, master. I didn't go far. Putting on this doctor's gown is like taking medicine. It works the same as a laxative.

DON JUAN Damn your excuses! Find a better covering for your cowardice. Do you realize whose life I saved before?

SGANARELLE I don't.

DON JUAN Elvire's brother.

SGANARELLE Her —

DON JUAN A pleasant man. He treated me fairly. I regret we're at odds.

SGANARELLE It's easy for you to settle things peacefully.

DON JUAN Yes, but I have no passion left for Doña Elvire, and I'm in no mood to marry her. You know how I must be free to love, not to lock my heart up inside four walls. As I've told you many times, I follow the line of least resistance toward whatever appeals to me. Every beautiful woman deserves a share of my affections. It's up to each one to take her turn and hold on to them for as long as she can . . . Look — what is that imposing structure I see between the trees?

SGANARELLE You don't recognize it?

DON JUAN No I don't.

SGANARELLE Well! That's the tomb the Commander was putting up for himself when you killed him.

DON JUAN You're right. I didn't know it was near here. I've been told so much about it. Very impressive, I hear, and so is his statue. I'd like to look at it close up.

SGANARELLE Don't go in, master.

DON JUAN   Why not?

SGANARELLE   It's not polite to visit a man you've killed.

DON JUAN   On the contrary, I'll pay my respects. And he should welcome me graciously if he's a gentleman. Let's go inside.

The tomb opens. Inside: a superb mausoleum and the Commander's statue.

SGANARELLE   That's really nice. Nice statues. Nice marble. Nice columns. Very nice all around. Don't you think so?

DON JUAN   A dead man couldn't wish for anything more ambitious. What strikes me is that a man who was happy with a simple home when he was alive should want so elaborate a home when he can't enjoy it.

SGANARELLE   Here's the Commander's statue.

DON JUAN   Splendid! The costume of a Roman emperor. Very suitable!

SGANARELLE   Great workmanship. So realistic. He looks alive and ready to speak. I'd be nervous if I was on my own, the way he's staring down. I wouldn't say he's pleased to see us.

DON JUAN   That's very wrong of him when I've come to pay my respects. Ask him if he'll join me for supper.

SGANARELLE   I'd say that's one thing he doesn't need.

DON JUAN   Ask him, I tell you.

SGANARELLE   You're not serious? Talk to a statue? I'm not crazy.

DON JUAN   Do as you're told.

SGANARELLE   This is spooky! My lord Commander . . . *(Aside)* Can't help laughing. I feel like a fool. But my master insists. . . *(Aloud)*   My lord Commander, my master Don Juan asks whether you will do him the honor of joining him for supper. *(The Statue nods.)* Oo-ah!

DON JUAN   What's wrong with you? Speak up!

SGANARELLE   *(Nodding like the Statue)*   The Statue . . .

DON JUAN   Yes? What are you trying to say?

SGANARELLE   I saw the Statue . . .

DON JUAN   So? You saw the Statue. And? Speak or I'll flatten you.

SGANARELLE   The Statue gave me a sign.

DON JUAN   You shivering idiot!

SGANARELLE   It did! Gave me a sign. A real nod. See for yourself. Talk to him and maybe —

DON JUAN   Watch this. I'll show you how gutless you are. Pay attention. My lord Commander, will you join me for supper?

The Statue nods again.

SGANARELLE   I wouldn't have missed that for ten gold coins. Well, master?

DON JUAN   Come! Out of this place . . .

SGANARELLE   So much for your bold unbelievers.

ACT FOUR

Don Juan, Sganarelle, and Ragotin in a room in Don Juan's home.

DON JUAN   Whatever it was, let's leave it at that, nothing unusual
— the dim lighting, which misled us, or a sudden giddy sensation,
which distorted our vision.

SGANARELLE   Master, don't try to deny what we saw with our own
eyes. Nothing could have been plainer than that nod of the head. I
feel certain that God, who's appalled by your goings-on, showed
you a miracle to convince you to stop and —

DON JUAN   Listen. If you keep nagging at me with your stupid
morality, if you say one more word about it, I'll send for a bullwhip
and three or four men to hold you down, and I'll flog you one
thousand times. Is that clear?

SGANARELLE   Crystal clear, master. You explain yourself with
such lucidity. That's what I like about you. You don't quibble.
You say what's on your mind, all the essential details.

DON JUAN   Have them bring in my supper as soon as possible.
Ragotin, my chair!

Enter La Violette.

LA VIOLETTE   Master, that merchant Monsieur Dimanche wants to
speak to you.

SGANARELLE   Great, that's all we need, a call from a creditor.
What makes him think he can stroll in here asking for money? Why
didn't you tell him the master's not home?

LA VIOLETTE   I did, for three-quarters of an hour. He doesn't
believe it. He sat down inside there to wait.

SGANARELLE   He can wait as long as he wants.

DON JUAN Not at all. Send him in. Avoiding your creditors is a bad policy. It's better to make some payment. I know a way to send them off satisfied without giving them a penny.

Enter Monsieur Dimanche, escorted by flunkeys.

DON JUAN *(With great civility)* Ah, Dimanche, do come in. I'm delighted to see you and furious with my servants for not bringing you here right away. I ordered them not to admit anyone, but the order does not apply to you. To you my door is always open.

MONSIEUR DIMANCHE I'm very grateful, monsieur.

DON JUAN *(To his lackeys)* Ruffians, how dare you keep Dimanche waiting in the hallway! I'll teach you to recognize my friends.

MONSIEUR DIMANCHE It was nothing, monsieur.

DON JUAN Nothing? Saying I was out to my closest friend!

MONSIEUR DIMANCHE Your servant, monsieur. I've come to —

DON JUAN Quick, here: a chair for Dimanche!

MONSIEUR DIMANCHE I'm all right here, monsieur.

DON JUAN Not at all. I want you to sit next to me.

MONSIEUR DIMANCHE That's not necessary.

DON JUAN Remove this stool! Bring him an armchair!

MONSIEUR DIMANCHE Don't bother, monsieur, to —

DON JUAN No bother. I'm aware how much I owe you, and I'll have no distinction made between us.

MONSIEUR DIMANCHE Monsieur —

DON JUAN Come, sit down.

MONSIEUR DIMANCHE There's no need to, monsieur. I want a quick word with you. I was —

DON JUAN   Sit down there, will you?

MONSIEUR DIMANCHE   I'm fine as I am, monsieur. I came to —

DON JUAN   No, I won't listen till you sit.

MONSIEUR DIMANCHE   *(Sitting)* As you wish, monsieur. I —

DON JUAN   God in heaven, Dimanche, you do look well.

MONSIEUR DIMANCHE   Yes, monsieur. Thank you, monsieur.
I'm here to —

DON JUAN   Fit as a fiddle, eh? Red lips, fresh cheeks, and bright
eyes.

MONSIEUR DIMANCHE   I'd like to —

DON JUAN   How is your wife?

MONSIEUR DIMANCHE   Very well, monsieur, praise God.

DON JUAN   A lovable woman.

MONSIEUR DIMANCHE   She'd thank you for that, monsieur. I'm
hoping to —

DON JUAN   And little Claudine, your daughter?

MONSIEUR DIMANCHE   As well as can be.

DON JUAN   What a pretty girl! I love her dearly.

MONSIEUR DIMANCHE   You're too kind, monsieur. Could you —?

DON JUAN   How about young Colin? Is he still making all that din
banging on his drum?

MONSIEUR DIMANCHE   As much as ever, monsieur. I wonder —

DON JUAN   And your little dog, Barker? Does he still growl
ferociously and sink his teeth into the legs of your visitors?

MONSIEUR DIMANCHE   More than ever, monsieur. We don't know how to stop him.

DON JUAN   You won't be surprised that I ask after your family. I take a personal interest in them all.

MONSIEUR DIMANCHE   We're extremely grateful, monsieur. And I —

DON JUAN   *(Holding out his hand)*   Give me your hand on that, Dimanche. You do feel like one of my friends, don't you?

MONSIEUR DIMANCHE   I'm your servant, monsieur.

DON JUAN   God in heaven, I'm so fond of you!

MONSIEUR DIMANCHE   You're too kind. I —

DON JUAN   There's nothing I wouldn't do for you.

MONSIEUR DIMANCHE   I'm deeply obliged to you, monsieur.

DON JUAN   And not for selfish reasons, believe me.

MONSIEUR DIMANCHE   I don't deserve the compliment. But monsieur —

DON JUAN   Let's drop the formality, Dimanche. Will you join me for supper?

MONSIEUR DIMANCHE   No, monsieur, I must get back right away. I —

DON JUAN   *(Standing)*   Quick, a torch for Dimanche! Four or five of you, take your muskets and escort him home.

MONSIEUR DIMANCHE   *(Standing)*   No need for all that, monsieur. I can manage very well on my own. But —

Sganarelle promptly takes out the chairs.

DON JUAN   Please! I want you to have an escort. You mean a great deal to me. I'm at your service, and also in your debt.

MONSIEUR DIMANCHE Exactly, monsieur, and —

DON JUAN I wouldn't hide it. I tell everyone.

MONSIEUR DIMANCHE If —

DON JUAN Would you like me to walk you outside?

MONSIEUR DIMANCHE Ah, monsieur, that's more than I —

DON JUAN Very well, then. A brotherly embrace . . . Please! *(Embracing him)* Remember, call on me at any time for anything. I am unequivocally yours. *(Exit.)*

SGANARELLE I must say the master's very attached to you.

MONSIEUR DIMANCHE True. He's so polite and affable I'll never be able to ask for my money.

SGANARELLE He's not the only one. Every person in this household would go the limit for you. I only wish someone would try to do you harm, beat you up, let's say. You'd soon see how we'd die before we —

MONSIEUR DIMANCHE I believe you. But Sganarelle, couldn't you please put in a word for me about my money?

SGANARELLE Don't worry. He'll pay you unequivocally.

MONSIEUR DIMANCHE And you, Sganarelle? The amount you owe me?

SGANARELLE Poo! Let's not talk about that.

MONSIEUR DIMANCHE What? I —

SGANARELLE Don't I know what I owe you?

MONSIEUR DIMANCHE Yes, but —

SGANARELLE Come, Dimanche. *(Taking a torch)* I'll enlighten you.

MONSIEUR DIMANCHE But my money —?

SGANARELLE *(Taking his arm)* You don't mean it?

MONSIEUR DIMANCHE I want —

SGANARELLE *(Tugging him)* Here!

MONSIEUR DIMANCHE I understand —

SGANARELLE *(Pushing him)* Not worth mentioning.

MONSIEUR DIMANCHE But —

SGANARELLE *(Pushing him)* There!

MONSIEUR DIMANCHE I —

SGANARELLE *(Shoving him offstage)* There you go!

A scene break with curtain or lighting.

Don Juan and Sganarelle on stage. Enter La Violette.

LA VIOLETTE Monsieur, your father is here.

DON JUAN Perfect. Just what I need to send up my temperature.

Enter Don Louis.

DON LOUIS I can see I am embarrassing you. You would have preferred me not to come. The fact is, we grate on each other. If you are tired of the sight of me, I am just as tired of your conduct. Unfortunately, in our ignorance we fail to let God determine our needs; we think we know better than He does. Then we plague Him with our blind desires and ill-considered demands. How I wanted a son! How I implored — fervently, unceasingly! And this son, for whom I wearied God with my pleas, who was to delight and console me, instead vexes and torments me. What am I to make of your succession of dishonorable deeds? How can I put a decent face on so much wickedness? Must I keep straining the King's generosity, after I have exhausted my stock of credit with him, and that of my friends? You have fallen so low! Don't you blush to be unworthy of your birth? Have you any right, I must ask, to be proud of who you are? What have you ever done to earn the title of nobleman? Do you think it enough to bear a noble name and arms?

Can you bask in the lofty reputation of our blood line when you lead a life of infamy? No, no, birth means nothing without virtue. We share in our ancestors' glory only so long as we do our utmost to resemble them. The reflections of their greatness, falling on us, are a commitment: we will reciprocate by following their example; we will not fall away from their high standards if we wish to be judged their true heirs. You do not belong to the men from whom you descend. They reject you, and you cannot claim any advantage from their brilliant achievements. Just the reverse: those achievements show you up for what you are. They serve as a torch that lights up your disgrace for the whole world to see. A nobleman who lives by evil is a natural monster. The first title to nobility is rectitude. For me the name a man signs counts for much less than the actions he performs, and I esteem a farm-laborer's honest son more highly than a king's son who lives as you do.

DON JUAN   Take a seat, father; you'll be more comfortable talking.

DON LOUIS   No, I will not sit down or say any more, because I see that my words don't touch you. But I will tell you, my mockery of a son, that you have pushed my natural affection as a father beyond the limits. Sooner than you think, I will put a stop to your wickedness before God's wrath overtakes you. With your punishment I will wash away the shame of having given you birth. *(Exit.)*

DON JUAN   The sooner you drop dead the better. You had your turn. It infuriates me when fathers live as long as their sons. *(He sits in an armchair.)*

SGANARELLE   No, master, you're wrong.

DON JUAN   I'm wrong?

SGANARELLE   Master —

DON JUAN   *(Standing up)*   I am wrong?

SGANARELLE   Yes, master, you're wrong to have put up with what he said. You should have grabbed him and turned him out. What a nerve! A father comes and chews out his son, tells him to mend his ways, remember his birth, lead a proper life, and all that other rubbish! And to a man like you who knows how to live — how could you swallow it? Your patience amazes me. If I were you,

I'd have sent him on his way, fast. *(Aside)* Curse this obedience!
I'm lower than the lowest.

DON JUAN   Will they bring in my supper?

Enter Ragotin.

RAGOTIN   Monsieur, this lady wearing a veil wants to speak to you.

DON JUAN   Who can it be?

SGANARELLE   We'll have to see.

Enter Doña Elvire.

DONA ELVIRE   Are you surprised, Don Juan, to see me at this hour
and in these clothes? I had to come and speak to you without delay.
I am no longer incensed, as I was this morning, no longer the Doña
Elvire who railed against you, threatened you, and swore
vengeance. God has lifted from my heart all traces of my unseemly
passion for you, all those excesses of a sinful infatuation, that
demeaning exhibition of crude, worldly love. He has purified my
love for you, cleansed it of its sensuality, left it sacred, detached,
unselfish, intending only what is best for you.

DON JUAN   *(To Sganarelle)*   You're weeping, I think.

SGANARELLE   I'm sorry.

DONA ELVIRE   This untainted love brings me here, in your interest,
to let you know the will of heaven and try to win you back from the
brink of doom, which you have now reached. Yes, Don Juan, I
know of all the disorder in your life. And yet God, Who touched
my heart and showed me my own errors, has inspired me to visit
you and say that your offenses have used up His mercy. His
terrible wrath is about to overwhelm you, unless you promptly
repent. You may now have less than one day in which to shield
yourself from the greatest of all misfortunes. As for me, I am no
longer bound to you in an earthly sense. I have turned away from
my folly, thanks be to Him. I am going into seclusion. I hope for
nothing more than enough time to atone for my sins and earn
forgiveness by devout penance for my impulsive and deplorable
passion. In my seclusion I will grieve deeply if a person who has
been very dear to me becomes a fatal example of God's justice. But

what joy I will feel if I can persuade you to avert the terrifying punishment that hangs over you! I implore you, Don Juan, as a final favor: grant me this gentle consolation. Don't refuse me. Respond to my tears and be saved! If you cannot act for your own good, at least act in answer to my prayers. Spare me the anguish of seeing you condemned to everlasting torment!

SGANARELLE *(Aside)* Poor woman!

DONA ELVIRE I loved you with all my being, above all else in the world. For you I turned away from my duty. Everything I have done I did for you. In return, I ask you to remake your life and escape destruction. If these tears from a woman you have loved are not enough, I plead in the name of whatever can move you.

SGANARELLE *(Aside, looking at Don Juan)* Heart of a tiger!

DONA ELVIRE Now I am leaving. I have said what I came to say.

DON JUAN It's late, madame. Stay over. We will give you the best room we have.

DONA ELVIRE No, Don Juan. You must not detain me.

DON JUAN Madame, I assure you I'd be very pleased if you would stay.

DONA ELVIRE I repeat: no. Let us not waste time with useless talk. I'll go quickly. Don't find any pretext for showing me out. Only heed my advice. *(Exit.)*

DON JUAN You know, I did feel something for her. Very interesting. New and bizarre. Her sloppy dress, her lovelorn air, and her tears started to bring the old, dead fires back to life.

SGANARELLE But what she said had no effect on you?

DON JUAN Supper! now!

SGANARELLE Very good.

DON JUAN *(Sitting at the table)* Still, Sganarelle, we must consider how to reform.

SGANARELLE   That's it!

DON JUAN   That *is* it! How to reform. Another twenty or thirty years of living this way, and then we'll consider what we should do.

SGANARELLE   Oh!

DON JUAN   What do you say to that?

SGANARELLE   Not a thing. Here's supper.

Ragotin and La Violette bring in the dishes. From one of them Sganarelle takes a morsel and pops it in his mouth.

DON JUAN   Your cheek looks swollen. What is it? Tell me, what have you got there?

SGANARELLE   Not a thing.

DON JUAN   Show me. Horrible — a lump on his cheek. Quick, a knife: we must lance it. The poor lad can't stand the pain, and the abscess could stifle him. See: it's ready to burst. Why, you rascal!

SGANARELLE   No, master, I was just checking that the cook hadn't put in too much salt or pepper.

DON JUAN   Sit down here. Let's eat. After supper I have a task for you. You look hungry.

SGANARELLE   *(Sitting at the table)*   I'll say. I haven't eaten since this morning, master. Taste this: it's first class. *(As he starts to load his plate the servants remove it.)* My plate, my plate! Take it easy, will you? Good grief, you're too quick, my young friend, with the clean plates. And you, La Violette, you little hustler, are you serving invisible wine?

While one servant fills Sganarelle's glass, the other servant takes away his plate again.

A thumping at the door.

DON JUAN   Who knocked like that?

SGANARELLE   Who the hell is interrupting our meal?

DON JUAN   I want to dine in peace. Let nobody in.

SGANARELLE   Let me see who it is.

He goes to the door and returns trembling.

DON JUAN   What's wrong? Who is it?

SGANARELLE   The *(He nods like the Statue)* . . . is there.

DON JUAN   Let me see. I'll show that nothing can shake me.

SGANARELLE   Poor Sganarelle, where can you hide?

The Statue enters and sits at the table.

DON JUAN   Quick, another chair and place setting. Sganarelle, sit down again.

SGANARELLE   Master, I'm not hungry now.

DON JUAN   Sit, I said. And drink — to the Commander's health. Fill Sganarelle's glass.

SGANARELLE   Master, I'm not thirsty.

DON JUAN   Drink, and let's have a song to entertain the Commander.

SGANARELLE   Master, I have a cold.

DON JUAN   That doesn't matter. Sing up! *(Sganarelle croaks a few notes.)* You others, bring instruments and accompany him.

THE STATUE   Don Juan, that will do. I return your invitation. Will you have supper with me tomorrow? Are you bold enough to come?

DON JUAN   Yes. I'll be there with only Sganarelle.

SGANARELLE   Many thanks, but tomorrow I have to fast.

DON JUAN   Sganarelle, take this torch and show —

THE STATUE   We need no light when guided by God.

ACT FIVE

A country setting. Don Louis, Don Juan, Sganarelle.

DON LOUIS   My son, can God have bountifully answered my prayers? Is this true, what you say? You are not leading me on with false hopes? How can I believe in this sudden conversion?

DON JUAN   *(Hypocritically)*   Yes, as you will see, I have turned away from my errors. I forswear what I was last night. In a flash God brought about a change in me that will astound the world. He touched my soul and opened my eyes. I now look back with horror on my long blindness and my crimes. As I reflect on those unspeakable acts, I marvel that He bore them for so long without raining down dire punishments on my head. I have come to appreciate His mercy and restraint. I will now profit from them and do what I should. Let everyone witness this transformation, watch how I make up for the scandals in my past life, and try to deserve His full forgiveness. As I strive for that end, I ask you, father, to assist me in choosing a person to guide me along the path I must take.

DON LOUIS   My son, it is easy to reawaken a father's love. His son's offenses evaporate at the first penitent word. I am already forgetting all the pains I have suffered on your account, thanks to what you have just said. I am so happy! — do you see these tears of joy? God has granted me what I prayed for; I ask for nothing more. Embrace me, my son, and let me urge you to follow through with this admirable effort. I must immediately share the wonderful news and my delight with your mother, and thank the good Lord for inspiring you to make these pious resolutions   *(Exit.)*

SGANARELLE   Master, I can't tell you how pleased I am to see you converted. I've been waiting so long for that, and now, thank God, my wishes have come true.

DON JUAN   Oh, this imbecile!

SGANARELLE   Which imbecile?

DON JUAN Do you take what I said at face value? Do you think you heard my heart when I opened my mouth?

SGANARELLE What! It wasn't . . .? You didn't . . .? You haven't . . .? Oh! *(Aside)* What a man! what a man! what a man!

DON JUAN No, I haven't changed at all. My old feelings remain intact.

SGANARELLE You're not a bit intimidated by that miracle of a statue that moves and speaks?

DON JUAN There is definitely something about it I don't understand. But whatever it is, it cannot influence the way I think or feel. I said I wanted to reform and lead a model life out of pure expedience, as a useful trick, a posture to win over my father, whom I may need, and also as a safeguard against the many misadventures in which people may entangle me. I'm confiding in you, Sganarelle, because I very much want one witness to my true beliefs and motives.

SGANARELLE So you still don't believe in anything, and yet you hope to present yourself as an honest man?

DON JUAN Why not? There's a multitude like me. They dabble in the same business and wear the same mask for their own advancement.

SGANARELLE *(Aside)* Oh what a man! What a man!

DON JUAN These days hypocrisy is nothing to be ashamed of. It's a fashionable vice, and vices pass for virtues after they come into fashion. The honest man is the finest role you can pick today, and so the professional hypocrite starts out with striking advantages. The art of imposture enjoys wide respect. Even people who recognize it for what it is don't dare speak up. All other vices can be openly condemned and attacked; but hypocrisy is a vice with privileges. It shoves its fist into the mouth of its critics. It thrives as unassailably as a monarch. It amounts to a tight society, a party or a religion made up of people who know one another's language or signs. If you attack one of them, all the others descend on you. There are, of course, men who are genuinely honest and devout. But they get taken in by the impostors and even join the ranks. There, in their pride and blindness, they prop up the very villains who are aping their honesty. I know many a man who has availed himself of the tactics of hypocrisy in order to cover up the damages of a misspent youth. He buckles the cloak of piety around him and, under that respected cloth, is immune — free to do as much evil as he can. It doesn't help to see through such people and know them for what they are. Society still accepts them for what they pretend to be. They bow their heads, let out mortified sighs, roll their eyes a couple of times, and lo, all is forgiven. I want to enter that shelter and be safe to carry on with my affairs. I do not plan to give up my pleasurable way of life, but I will take care to keep it hidden and quiet. If ever I am found out, I won't need to defend myself; I'll let the rest of the cabal rise up and take my part against anyone who criticizes me. You see, this is the best way to do what I want while I avoid punishment. I will appoint myself a censor of other people's actions, pronounce the rest of the world bad, and have a good opinion of . . . myself only. If any man upsets me, however slightly, I will never forgive him but will feed and water my grudge. I will become the spokesman for God's revenge, and with this convenient excuse, I will assault my enemies and accuse them of being irreligious. Against them I will launch those zealous busybodies who are willing to attack anyone in public with no excuse but the authority they have taken on themselves. This is how I will benefit from human weakness and draw up a sensible pact with the vices of our age.

SGANARELLE Good God! Now what are you saying? That you've added hypocrisy to your list of sins? That's all you needed to round you off — the worst, the most abominable crime. Master, for me this is the last straw. I'm bursting. I must speak. Do what you want to me, whip me, thrash me, kill me, if you must, but I'll get this out of my system, because as a loyal servant I owe it to you. Remember, master, the pitcher smashes when it goes to the well too many times; and as some author — I don't know which one — has said, man is like a bird clinging to a bough; the bough clings to the tree; and anyone who clings to the tree follows good precepts; good precepts are worth more than fine words; you hear fine words at the court; at the court you find courtiers; courtiers observe the fashions; fashions arise from our fantasies; our fantasies arise from the soul; the soul is the source of life; life ends with death; death makes us think of heaven; heaven is above the earth; the earth is not the sea; at sea there are storms; storms can wreck ships; a ship needs a good pilot; a good pilot has prudence; prudence is absent from the young; the young must obey the old; the old love wealth; wealth makes them rich; the rich are not poor; the poor suffer from poverty;

against poverty there's no law; without law, men are wild beasts; and consequently, you're as damned as all the devils.

DON JUAN   A powerful argument!

SGANARELLE   If you don't act on it, all the worse for you.

Enter Don Carlos.

DON CARLOS   Don Juan, it's lucky that I met you here, rather than in your home, to ask what you have decided. You heard me undertake to settle this matter. I'll be candid. I would prefer a friendly agreement. To bring that about I will be glad to see you confirm in public that my sister is your wife.

DON JUAN   *(Hypocritically)*   Oh dear! I wish with all my heart that I could meet your desires. But God will not have it so. He has inspired me to remake myself. I am now resolved to give up all worldly attachments; to shed all tokens of vanity as swiftly as possible; and to rectify the crimes of my fiery, heedless youth by leading a life of self-denial.

DON CARLOS   That purpose, Don Juan, does not clash with my proposal. Taking a lawful wife is quite consistent with the admirable ideas inspired in you by our Lord.

DON JUAN   I am afraid not. Your sister has come to the identical decision. She has made up her mind to go into seclusion. We were both moved at the same time by the same divine grace.

DON CARLOS   That does not satisfy us. Her seclusion might seem to be the result of your contempt for her and for our family. Our honor requires that she live with you as your wife.

DON JUAN   That, I assure you, is not possible. It happens to be what I wanted most. Only today I sought the Lord's advice; but after my supplications a voice told me I must put your sister out of my thoughts, for with her I could never find my salvation.

DON CARLOS   Don Juan, do you think you can hoodwink us with these excuses?

DON JUAN   I am obeying the voice from heaven.

DON CARLOS   Do you expect to fob me off with that sort of talk?

DON JUAN   God wills it.

DON CARLOS   You removed my sister from the convent only to forsake her?

DON JUAN   God commands it.

DON CARLOS   Are we to tolerate this slur on our family name?

DON JUAN   You must appeal to God.

DON CARLOS   What is this God and God and God?

DON JUAN   God requires it.

DON CARLOS   Enough, Don Juan, I understand you. This is not a suitable place for settling our dispute. But I will shortly find you again.

DON JUAN   As you wish. You are aware that I do not lack courage and know how to use my sword when necessary. I shall soon pass along the alley that leads to the main convent house. I assure you that I have no desire to fight. God has forbidden me. But if you begin the attack, we shall see what comes of it.

DON CARLOS   We shall. We certainly shall see.   *(Exit.)*

SGANARELLE   Master, what's this new manner of yours? It's worse than your others. I'd even prefer you the way you were before. I was still hoping you could be saved; but now my hopes are dead, and I believe that God, Who has put up with you for so long, won't be able to stand this last atrocity.

DON JUAN   Come on, come on, God is not as strict as you think. If men were punished for every —

A Specter appears as a veiled woman.

SGANARELLE   Master, see! God has sent a warning.

DON JUAN   When God warns me, He'll have to speak more plainly if He wants me to hear.

THE SPECTER   Don Juan has almost no time left to profit from God's mercy. If he does not repent now he is lost.

SGANARELLE   You did hear that, master?

DON JUAN   Who dares speak those words? Do I recognize that voice?

SGANARELLE   No, master, it's a ghost. I can see by its walk.

DON JUAN   Ghost, spirit, or devil, I'll find out what it is.

The Specter changes shape, and becomes Time holding a scythe.

SGANARELLE   Oh God, did you see that, master, how it changed its shape?

DON JUAN   Nothing can frighten me. My sword will soon tell me if it's a body or a spirit.

The Specter vanishes before Don Juan can strike it.

SGANARELLE   Quick, master, give way before all this evidence. Repent fast!

DON JUAN   No. Whatever happens, it shall never be said that I could repent. Come.

The Statue enters.

THE STATUE   Don Juan! Wait! Yesterday you promised to join me for supper.

DON JUAN   Yes. Which way do we go?

THE STATUE   Give me your hand.

DON JUAN   Here.

THE STATUE   Don Juan, the hardened sinner earns a terrifying death, and spurning God's mercy invites the thunderbolt.

DON JUAN   Oh my God, what is this agony? The scorching of fires within — unbearable! My whole body is ablaze. Ahhh!

A crash of thunder and bolts of lightning fall on Don Juan. The ground opens and swallows him. Great flames leap from the place where he disappeared.

SGANARELLE   But my pay! My pay! . . . In the end his death delights them all: an offended Almighty, broken laws, violated girls, dishonored families, outraged parents, seduced wives, enraged husbands . . . Everybody's satisfied. Except me. All those years of service, and my only remuneration is to watch my sinful master undergo the most gruesome punishment I can imagine. . . My pay! My pay! My pay!

The end of

Don Juan

Postscript

Both plays in this book are set in Southern Italy, *Scapin* in Naples and *Don Juan* in an unspecified part of Sicily during the rule of Spain. Yet both plays are saturated in Frenchness. How, then, does one translate the names? Frank Dunlop found an ingenious answer with his *Scapino.* He Italianized the names and the title, took the characters and their *lazzi* and *burli* back to their commedia dell'arte origins, and came up with a British pantomime that poked fun at its own Italian pretensions. Other translators and adapters have variously kept the location or predominant tone or cultural ambience in France (as in this version) or given it a British or American tilt. However one copes with these details, *Scapin,* a farce, follows a consistent line.

Don Juan does not. For a translator it is the most daunting of Molière's prose plays, although his mightiest. I apologize to readers and performers for the jumble of Spanish titles (Don, Doña), English titles (the Commander, the Statue, the Specter), and French versions of Spanish names (Elvire, Alonse), a compromise reached after long indecision. Perhaps that compromise can be justified by pointing out that the play itself is not only international in character but also a curious mixture. It blends the natural and the unnatural with the supernatural. It incorporates comedy, farce, tragedy, and melodrama; a few French peasants with their French names, Spanish-derived characters, not all of them borrowed from Tirso de Molina's *The Trickster of Seville;* and Sganarelle, Molière's own role, who is as much of an apparent anomaly here as Puck is in *A Midsummer Night's Dream.* The playwright may have intended to impose some consistency on these varied components by his choice of setting. Did he know that Sicily was the home of Epicharmus, the comic writer of antiquity, and, as some scholars believe, of the earliest Greek farcical mime performances called the *phlyakes?* If so, Molière was possibly implying that in the play, which carries no subtitle to define its genre, the comic and farcical elements should overpower the bitter and tragic ones. He seems to support this speculation by giving Sganarelle the lines that open and close the play, as well as the final words in the first, second, and third acts, and by keeping that earnest, two-faced duffer onstage for twenty-six of the play's twenty-seven scenes, while Don Juan appears in twenty-five.

Whatever Molière knew or intended, Sicily was not Paris (much as Venice was not London for Shakespeare and Jonson). On that foreign soil he could plant home truths like the ones in Juan's Act Five speech about hypocrisy, frustrating his enemies and detractors by making them recognizable yet not quite identifiable.

The language of Elvire, Louis, Carlos, and Alonse, almost as formal and as elegantly graded in the thought progressions as Corneille's verse tirades, contrasts with the Beauce dialect of Charlotte and Pierrot (the latter another refugee from the commedia). But Charlotte assumes a milder dialect during her colloquies with Juan as she tries to speak more "nicely." Juan in his turn shifts between the gallant precision of his peers and his father and a sarcastic bluntness in his scenes with Sganarelle. Sganarelle differs again. He has a broadly comic personality and his arguments are either ridiculed by Juan or patently ridiculous, especially his long and muddily mercurial speech on conformity in Act 5; but although ill-educated he is no illiterate, and at times he has to convey an underlying seriousness in order to function as Juan's principal antagonist.

The formal speeches give a translator the big headaches. They will not go into a stage English that releases the flow of narrative beauty of the French. Strict accuracy often results in lengthily cryptic utterances or even unintelligibility. I have frequently had to rephrase in order to escape from Molière's sentence structure, and am praying that his statue will not knock and invite me to supper.

To that master scholar, critic, playwright, and translator Eric Bentley I am unrepayably indebted for his correspondence and our conversations. To Joyce, my wife, I am indebted for just about everything.

Albert Bermel
The Bronx, New York, 1987.

THE BEST SHORT PLAYS
1987
Edited by Ramon Delgado

LIFE UNDER WATER
Richard Greenberg

WORMWOOD
Amlin Gray

GOIN' WEST
Louis Phillips

HOW GERTRUDE STORMED
THE PHILOSOPHER'S CLUB
Martin Epstein

SPITTIN' IMAGE
Stephen Metcalf

A BETROTHAL
Lanford Wilson

HOW IT HANGS
Grace McKeaney

PRACTICAL MAGIC
Shannon Keith Kelley

WHY THE LORD CAME TO
SAND MOUNTAIN
Romulus Linney

THE STONEWATER RAPTURE
Doug Wright

$10.95 (paper) ISBN: 0-936839-94-5
$18.95 (cloth) ISBN: 0-936839-95-3

"Acting, Directing, Text Analysis, Playwriting—any course which intersects today's theatre will find the new inexpensive Applause format to be an invaluable resource."

—Howard Stein
Columbia University

"An important step forward in the development of the most exciting new writers of dramatic literature and a timely reminder of the towering talent of some of our already established dramatists."

—World Literature Today

"There is pure excitement in these plays! Should you buy this collection for your personal library? Of course. Should you insist that your school and town libraries include the whole series in their holdings? CERTAINLY!"

—Dramatics Magazine

"These are sharp, tightly constructed pieces with small casts, as readable as they are actable—just the sort of thing community players and other small ensembles will find practical."

—Booklist

THE BEST SHORT PLAYS
1986

$10.95 (paper) ISBN: 0-936839-13-9
$18.95 (cloth) ISBN: 0-936839-14-7

APPLAUSE
THEATRE BOOK PUBLISHERS

THE APPLAUSE ACTING SERIES
An Innovative System of Texts and Techniques
General Editors: Michael Earley and Philippa Keil

Whether preparing for an audition, a scene study class, a production, or a career, the Applause Acting Series tells actors exactly what they need to know in a language and format they can easily understand. Each volume is designed to challenge and support the serious beginner and expand the horizons of the experienced professional actor.

THE STANISLAVSKY TECHNIQUE: RUSSIA
A Workshop for Actors
by Mel Gordon   New York University

Stop reading about Stanislavsky and wondering what it's all supposed to mean. Meet the master and his disciples as they evolve new techniques and exercises in a workshop atmosphere over a quarter of a century.

This Volume Includes:
The Stanislavsky System: First Studio Exercises: 1912-1916
Vakhtangov as Rebel and Theortician: Exercises 1919-1921
Michael Chekhov: Exercises 1919-1952
Stanislavsky's Fourth Period: Theory of Physical Actions: 1934-1938

Bibliography $ 8.95 (paper) ISBN: 0-936839-08-2
            $18.95 (cloth) ISBN: 0-936839-09-0

THE STANISLAVSKY TECHNIQUE: AMERICA
A Workshop for Actors
by Mel Gordon   New York University

Attend the Workshops, perform the exercises of every major acting teacher in America since Stanislavsky.

This Volume Includes:
American Lab Theatre and Boleslavsky: Exercises 1924-1929
The Group Theatre: Exercises 1931-1941
The Actor's Lab in Hollywood: Exercises 1941-1948
Stella Adler and the Adler Conservatory: Exercises 1949-1986
The Actor's Studio: 1947-1956
Bobby Lewis and The Lewis Studio: Exercises 1962-1986
Sandy Meisner at The Neighborhood Playhouse: Exercises 1957-1986
Lee Strasberg and The Strasberg Institute: Exercises 1962-1980

$ 8.95 (paper) ISBN: 0-936839-10-4
$18.95 (cloth) ISBN: 0-936839-11-2

APPLAUSE
THEATRE BOOK PUBLISHERS

ANCIENT COMEDY ROARS BACK TO LIFE!

CLASSICAL COMEDY GREEK AND ROMAN

Edited by Robert W. Corrigan

The only book of its kind: For the first time Greek *and* Roman masters of comedy meet in this extraordinary new forum devised and edited by a master scholar of comedy himself, Robert Corrigan. Corrigan has enlisted six superb translations to create an unmatched Olympiad of classical comedy.

Be prepared to exercise your social conscience, your funny bone, your mind, your sides, and don't be surprised if you find yourself in the aisles. You won't be alone. Neil Simon, William Shakespeare, Feydeau, Woody Allen, George Bernard Shaw, Mel Brooks, Noel Coward, Pirandello, Monty Python, and Alan Ayckbourn, to name but a few, are all there in the galleries, observing, miming, taking notes. So, take note: The laugh you hear today got its start centuries before the birth of Christ and represents the most virulent strain of drama in the western tradition. The six introductions which accompany the plays constitute in themselves a valuable colloquium on the ancient art of comedy and its potent influence today.

ARISTOPHANES	LYSISTRATA
	translated by Donald Sutherland
	THE BIRDS
	translated by Walter Kerr
MENANDER	THE GROUCH
	translated by Sheila D'Atri
PLAUTUS	THE MENAECHMI
	translated by Palmer Bovie
	THE HAUNTED HOUSE
	translated by Palmer Bovie
TERENCE	THE SELF-TORMENTOR
	translated by Palmer Bovie

$8.95 (paper)
5 x 7¾, 596 pages
ISBN: 0-936839-85-6

APPLAUSE
THEATRE BOOK PUBLISHERS

François Truffaut

small change

"An original, a major work . . . lilting, marvelously funny and wise."
— Vincent Canby, The New York Times

A film novel With More than 50 Photographs
$6.95 (paper)
ISBN: 0-936839-51-1

THE 400 BLOWS

"The 400 Blows **is one of the most beautiful films that I have ever seen."** —Akira Kurosawa

With over 100 illustrations

$7.95 (paper)
ISBN: 0-936839-55-4

Day for Night

"Truffaut's Finest Film! It is Truffaut's valentine to the world of film-making." —Rex Reed, *The New York Daily News*

$7.95 (paper)
ISBN: 0-936839-56-2

The Complete Script of the Film With More than 50 Photographs

---

Michelangelo ANTONIONI

THE PASSENGER

" A superior suspense melodrama, probably Antonioni's most entertaining film."—Vincent Canby, *The New York Times.*

The Complete Script by Mark Peploe, Peter Wollen, and Michelangelo Antonioni

$6.95 (paper)
ISBN: 0-936839-52-X

With over 70 Photographs

I AM CURIOUS (yellow)

The complete scenario of the film by Vilgot Sjöman with over 250 illustrations

"One of the most important pictures I have ever seen in my life. . . I think it is a profoundly moral movie."
—Norman Mailer

$7.95 (paper)
ISBN: 0-936839-53-8

SAVAGES and SHAKESPEARE WALLAH

Two Films By James Ivory

"It is utterly unique in its subject matter and one can say of it, as one can of few films, that you have never seen anything quite like it."

— *Richard Schickel, Life*

$7.95 (paper)
ISBN: 0-936839-54-6

LA GUERRE EST FINIE

Scenario by Jorge Semprun For the film by Alain Resnais

$7.95 (paper)
ISBN: 0-936839-57-0

" Resnais' genius in movie-making is as important and distinctive as Faulkner's in the novel."
—Brendan Gill, *The New Yorker*

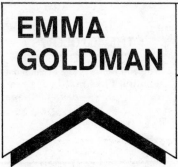

EMMA
GOLDMAN

THE SOCIAL
SIGNIFICANCE
OF MODERN DRAMA
Introduction by Harry G. Carlson

"HURRAH!" Now Emma Goldman's revolutionary book will be on everyone's shelf and in everyone's heart and on everyone's lips. And if only, if only, the message is made clear, then there may be some real hope."

—Judith Malina

"Learn what drama meant to one of the most remarkable women in American history."

—Eric Bentley

"This great book may have finally found the decade hungry for its profound truths. Emma Goldman's brave crusade reminds us that the theatre entertains us best when it calls forth visions of what is highest and best in us and undermines human hypocrisies, cruelties, and greed."

—Karen Malpede, Author
WOMEN IN THEATRE

Out of print virtually since its completion in 1914, Emma Goldman's pioneer work SOCIAL SIGNIFICANCE OF MODERN DRAMA bridges modern drama and political philosophy, pointing out the road that remains to be travelled toward a theatre of social empowerment. Activist, feminist, philosopher and anarchist, Emma Goldman was a passionate thinker about all things modern when the Twentieth Century was still raw and new. The emergence of her treatise on the theatre after years of obscurity is certain to arouse a new generation of artists and scholars with its timely and provocative vision.

"Ibsen, Strindberg, Hauptmann, Chekhov, Tolstoy, Shaw, Galsworthy and other dramatists contained in this volume represent the social iconoclasts of our time. They know that society has gone beyond the stage of patching up, and that man must throw off the dead weight of the past, with all its ghosts and spooks, if he is to go foot free into the future."
This is the social significance which differentiates modern dramatic art from art for art's sake. It is the dynamite which undermines superstition, shakes the social pillars, and prepares men and women for the reconstruction."

—Emma Goldman

$8.95 (paper) ISBN: 0-936839-61-9
$18.95 (cloth) ISBN: 0-936839-62-7
5½ x 8¼, 192 pages

APPLAUSE
THEATRE BOOK PUBLISHERS

Nineteenth-Century American Plays
Edited by Myron Matlaw

From Broadway to Topeka these four smash hits were the staples of the American dramatic repertoire. Their revival in this landmark collection will once again bring America to its feet!

"BRAVO! ESSENTIAL FOR ALL THOSE INTERESTED IN AMERICAN THEATRE."
—*Brooks McNamara*
Director
The Shubert Archive

(paper) $8.95
(cloth) $18.95

MARGARET FLEMING
James A. Herne

THE OCTOROON
Dion Boucicault

FASHION
Anna Cora Mowatt

RIP van WINKLE
Joseph Jefferson

THE THEATER OF BLACK AMERICANS
Edited by Errol Hill

From the origins of the Negro spiritual and the birth of the Harlem Renaissance to the emergence of a national black theater movement, THE THEATER OF BLACK AMERICANS offers a penetrating look at a black art form that has exploded into an American cultural institution.

$12.95 (paper)
ISBN: 0-936839-27-9
Introduction, Notes and Bibliography

Among the essays:

Some African Influences on the Afro-American Theater
  JAMES HATCH
Notes on Ritual in the New Black Theatre
  SHELBY STEELE
The Aesthetic of Modern Black Drama: From Mimesis to Methexis
  KIMBERLY W. BENSTON
The Lafayette Players
  SISTER M. FRANCESCA THOMPSON, O.S.F.
The Role of Blacks in the Federal Theatre, 1935-1939
  RONALD ROSS
The Negro Ensemble Company: A Transcendent Vision
  ELLEN FOREMAN

APPLAUSE
THEATRE BOOK PUBLISHERS

EDIEVAL
AND
TUDOR DRAMA

Edited and with introductions by
JOHN GASSNER

The rich tapestry of medieval belief, morality, and manners, shines through this comprehensive anthology of the twenty-four major plays that bridge the dramatic worlds of medieval and Tudor England. Here are the plays that paved the way to the Renaissance and Shakespeare. In John Gassner's extensively annotated collection, the plays regain their timeless appeal and display their truly international character and influence.

MEDIEVAL AND TUDOR DRAMA remains the indispensable chronicle of a dramatic heritage—the classical plays of Hrotsvitha, folk and ritual drama, the passion play, the great morality play EVERYMAN, the interlude, Tudor comedies RALPH ROISTER DOISTER and GAMMER GURTON'S NEEDLE, and the most famous of Tudor tragedies GORBODUC. Mr. Gassner's introductions and notes tell a tale of excellence and evolution too easily forgotten. The texts have been modernized for today's readers and those composed in Latin have been translated into English.

This exceptional volume of plays joins the growing list of companion volumes from APPLAUSE (see *Eric Bentley's Dramatic Repertoire*)—each at an affordable price.

$8.95 (paper)
ISBN: 0-936839-84-8

ORDER FOR FALL CLASSES NOW.

APPLAUSE
THEATRE BOOK PUBLISHERS

THE ACTOR'S MOLIÈRE

MOLIÈRE
A New Series of Translations for the Stage
by Albert Bermel

THE MISER & GEORGE DANDIN

"Bermel's Molière translations are, with those of Richard Wilbur, by far the most amusing we have."
—Eric Bentley

"Bermel is an expert translator with a fine feeling both for prose and verse and an unusual understanding of the stage."
—Robert Brustein

Volume 1: 128 pages, 5x7, $5.95 (paper)
ISBN: 0-936839-75-9

THE DOCTOR IN SPITE OF HIMSELF
&
THE BOURGEOIS GENTLEMAN

"Bermel has rendered Molière into an English that is speakable, playable, lively, witty, and natural."
—Lionel Abel

"This is the first translation of Molière that made me feel that Molière could have written in English."
—George Savage

Volume 2: 128 pages, 5x7, $5.95 (paper)
ISBN: 0-936839-77-5

SCAPIN & DON JUAN

"All of us must be grateful that a sympathetic and gifted translator, who is himself a talented dramatist, has turned his attention to Molière."
—Stanley Kauffman

Volume 3: 128 pages, 5x7, $5.95 (paper)
ISBN: 0-936839-80-5

APPLAUSE
THEATRE BOOK PUBLISHERS